Opioids for the Masses:
Big Pharma's War on Middle America
And the White Working Class

OPIOIDS
FOR THE MASSES

**Big Pharma's War on Middle America
And the White Working Class**

Trey Garrison
&
Richard McClure

ANTELOPE HILL PUBLISHING

Cover art by sswifty.
Edited by Taylor Young and Margaret Bauer.
Interior formatting by Margaret Bauer.

The authors can be contacted at:
treygarrison@protonmail.com

Antelope Hill Publishing
www.antelopehillpublishing.com

Paperback ISBN-13: 978-1-953730-89-3
Hardcover ISBN-13: 978-1-953730-91-6
EPUB ISBN-13: 978-1-953730-90-9

For we must all appear before the judgment seat of Christ, so that each of us may receive what is due us for the things done while in the body, whether good or bad.

2 Corinthians 5:10

Contents

Chapter 1: Lost in America...1

Chapter 2: The Blizzard...13

Chapter 3: A Town as a Corpse...............................25

Chapter 4: The Rot..41

Chapter 5: Fighting Back..55

Chapter 6: Never-Ending Battle..............................75

Chapter 7: Among the Culprits................................85

Chapter 8: Too Close to Home.................................99

Chapter 9: Doctor Feelgood....................................111

Chapter 10: The Big Bad...110

Chapter 11: Lawyers, Drugs, and Money...............135

Chapter 12: Let Justice Be Done.............................143

Bibliography...149

1
Lost in America

In the rolling hills and hard mountains of Appalachia it feels like even on the best days you only get sunlight overhead for six hours. These mountains aren't high, but the valleys run deep, and the hollows where the locals live are close and intimate. The sun has long retreated behind the western ridge and a cool dampness has settled in this valley. We've turned off a state highway onto what the navigation says is a county road. It's one lane and has more gravel than concrete. The car is on about a 20-degree grade winding downward into the darkness. This road feels more like a driveway, and in a way, it is.

We're in Eastern Kentucky, trying to find the home of a former OxyContin dealer. If we pull up to the wrong home or farm, or even the right one, we might get greeted by suspicious eyes and a loaded shotgun. We check the navigation again and we're definitely lost. And in that way, we aren't so different from the America we've come looking for.

The story we've come for began just two decades ago, when a new generation of "safer" opium-based painkillers triggered an onslaught of prescriptions in America. Tragically and inevitably, these prescriptions were followed by dependence and abuse. In the decades since, opioid overdoses have killed well over 400,000 Americans, closing in on half a million. The wave of prescription drug abuse led to a wave of heroin addiction. What started as legal opiate use has become a crisis of illicit drug abuse. Now, more than half of opioid deaths are caused by synthetic drugs like fentanyl, a chemical thousands of times stronger than heroin and powerful enough to kill in tiny concentrations. Beyond the death toll, at least two million Americans have become addicted. More Americans have died from opiates since the 1990s than died in the entirety of World War II. And more than three times as many Americans have been injured from opiates as soldiers were wounded during that same conflict.

Opiate addiction and death have become a depressing reality for working Americans and their families. Today, 54 percent of Americans know someone who died from a drug overdose. One in three will have a friend who dies from a drug overdose in their lifetime. And drug overdose is now the leading cause of death for Americans under fifty.

That's what brought us to this quiet valley on a weekday evening in rural Kentucky. We're searching for answers about what's happening and why. Who are the people most affected? When and why did they become addicted? Could it have been prevented? And now that it's happened, how can it be stopped? We're convinced there's a deeper story here. And we're venturing down into the woods to get our start finding it.

* * *

There's an old, usually misattributed, quote that holds, "one death is a tragedy, but a million is just a statistic." Apocryphal or not, there's truth to the idea. In the modern world, we're awash in a blizzard of numbers and data so often that it's easy to get lost in the snowstorm. It's easy to forget that there are thousands of personal stories of tragedy and loss hidden inside every such statistic. Then again, every once in a while, you come across a number that crystallizes reality and it can stop you cold.

For us it was this: According to data from the Center for Disease Control and Prevention, overdoses involving opioids killed more than

47,000 Americans in 2017. More than a third of those deaths involved legal, prescription opioids. In 2019, there were 81,000 drug overdose deaths, of which the CDC estimates more than 70 percent were opioid related.

The 2017 number was our hook. We started this project in early 2019 and at the time that was the latest data available. It was shocking.

By comparison, the Vietnam War lasted nineteen years and saw 58,000 Americans die, but in 2017, nearly as many Americans perished from opioid overdoses as in twenty years of war in Southeast Asia. If you include all narcotics, there were 70,237 drug overdose deaths in the United States in 2017, making that year deadlier for Americans than the Vietnam War, Gulf War, Iraq War, and the Afghanistan campaign combined.

And this crisis shows little signs of slowing.

Make no mistake, the bulk of these deaths comes from prescription drugs and synthetic opioids, like OxyContin, Percocet, and others, including the synthetic prescription drug fentanyl. Only half again as many Americans died from truly illegal narcotics like heroin.

The number of legal, prescribed opioids has declined since its peak in 2013, but the astronomical growth prior to that year makes recent declines seem insignificant. When people dependent on prescription opioids can't get legal prescriptions, they increasingly turn to more dangerous alternatives like black market fentanyl and heroin. This is why the number of overdose deaths have tragically continued to climb despite prescriptions declining.

Alcohol and drug abuse have long been a part of the human condition, but the pills that caused this crisis were flooded into parts of the country—rural, working-class communities—where drug use was largely frowned upon and marginalized. These pills were doctor recommended and the prescriptions they required brought an air of legitimacy to the use of opioids. Average Americans became addicted without knowing there was any risk. But opiates brought the same dependency and addiction that has always followed the large-scale use of opium derivatives.

Economic setbacks, depression, pain and struggle have always been part of the American story. Our communities have faced ruthless business interests, crime, poverty, economic decline, discrimination, and natural disaster. With limited exceptions, few of these appear to have been as destructive to the social fabric and to the hope we feel for the future. Despair is now simply a part of life in many of the areas of America hardest hit by the opioid epidemic today, whether you're talking about the hollows of Appalachia or small towns in the Rust Belt and the South.

* * *

Opium and its derivatives have been in America since at least the Gold Rush, when Chinese laborers brought the habit with them. Morphine, which is derived from opium but is ten times stronger, was widely used as a painkiller in the Civil War, and historians estimate that about 400,000 American soldiers on both sides became addicted by the war's end.

In the 1870s scientists tried to develop a less addictive form of morphine, and the result, ironically, was heroin. A cautionary tale, if ever there was one. Initial claims by nineteenth century physicians and drug companies led many to believe that heroin was a "safe" version of morphine. Strikingly similar claims would be made more than a century later, and our collective failure to learn the lessons of the past plays a large role in this narrative.

The use of opium peaked around the turn of the twentieth century, but at nothing like the scale of today's crisis. With the restrictions that came in the 1910s and 1920s, opiate use was all but banished to tiny pockets of the urban classes in primarily metropolitan locations. There was no widespread opioid or heroin epidemic during the subsequent Great Depression. The Appalachian people have always enjoyed the tipple of moonshine, but their ongoing economic struggles never created significant demand for opium derivatives. In the upheavals of the 1960s and 1970s, drug use grew among middle- and upper-class youth, but struggling middle class and working-class Americans still looked down their noses at heroin users.

That was then. Now heroin and other opiates are being trafficked to parts of the country that they only passed through on their way to the inner cities before. Now the biggest consumers are working class White people in rural areas. How did it come to this? We spoke to Brandeis University opioid policy expert Dr. Andrew Kolodny to get a sense of how to properly understand what has been happening.

"To start with, the correct way to frame the opioid crisis is an epidemic of opioid addiction," Kolodny told us. "The reason we're experiencing record overdose deaths and that we're seeing fentanyl and heroin in parts of the country we've never seen it before, and outbreaks of injection related diseases, and births of opioid dependent babies, is all because of the increase in opioid addiction coming from prescription opioids."

Noting the 900 percent increase in opioid addicts between 1997 and 2011, he said the majority of overdoses are among those already addicted. But this is by no means the whole story. "I have a friend who lost his daughter who was seventeen. It was the night before she was going to college, and she was at a party," Kolodny said. "She was experimenting for the first time and took an 80 mg OxyContin which is a very high dose. One pill, and Emily died.

"That said, I really don't agree with framing this as a 'drug abuse' crisis, because that implies we have a lot of people behaving badly and accidentally killing themselves while behaving badly and recreationally. Some people became addicted because they abused opioid prescriptions and liked the feeling, but more are dependent and continue to use opioids not because they feel good but because when they are not taking them they feel sick.

"The other thing I would just say is that I don't agree with calling it an 'epidemic of overdose deaths'—but to frame the issue around the deaths would be like referring to the AIDS crisis as an epidemic of pneumocystis pneumonia. AIDS was a crisis of HIV infection. This is a crisis of opioid addiction."

* * *

We now live in an America where working class, predominantly White, rural people whose parents and grandparents would have spat at the idea of shooting up are now living and dying with needles in their arms. And they are doing it in extremely large numbers. Many, including Dr. Kolodny, describe this as an "epidemic." But is it really an epidemic? The world "epidemic" implies a disease spreading naturally, due to some pathogen. The "pathogen" idea makes it easy to get caught up in debating the best strategies or treatments for combatting this "natural occurrence," just as you would an outbreak of the bird flu. It sounds inevitable. The only hope is to treat the disease and hope the "epidemic" subsides.

In truth, this crisis isn't about a naturally occurring pathogen infecting the population. Centuries ago, it was possible to claim ignorance about the effect opiates have on patients. But the lessons of history are easy to learn if only we'd look. This wasn't inevitable. There were guiding hands behind designing these drugs, obtaining regulatory approval, and marketing them to patients and doctors. Whether by plan or criminal negligence, this crisis wouldn't have occurred without human action. Something set this in motion. Someone in the long chain of events that got us here were derelict in their duties or knew what they were doing. Maybe both.

Because this has both human intervention and a human death toll, maybe the more correct lens to view this through is not that it is an epidemic, but rather a crime. If one patient is deliberately and knowingly administered a deadly drug, we might treat it as murder, but now that the death toll is over 400,000, we call it an "epidemic"? What changes an event from a crime to a public health issue?

The full human cost is not simply an accounting of the dead, but includes the impact of despair and hopelessness that follows in the wake of opiate addiction and abuse. There is, as Adam Smith said, "much ruin in a nation."

We began our investigation into this crisis by considering the places hardest hit by opiate addiction, overdoses, and deaths. To our surprise, the hardest hit areas were home to certain rural and working-class American communities—exactly those who had most successfully resisted drugs in the past.

The fact that "flyover America" is most affected by the crisis explains the relative paucity of coverage in the news. Rural White Americans are those least likely to receive sympathy from coastal media and politicians. Both the leadership of the left and right often take rural and working-class Americans for granted. But these Americans are part of the backbone of this country. They comprise a surprising percentage of our armed forces. They contribute a disproportionate amount to the Federal tax coffers. And historically, they have provided the labor that made America the industrial superpower of the modern world. Without them, America simply won't be the same.

* * *

Our investigation into this opioid catastrophe naturally starts here, in Appalachia where the impact of addiction has been felt the most. Located in the heart of the economically ravaged coal belt, this is where the opioid crisis really began. The path to addiction was paved on these country roads.

Coal mining is back-breaking labor and eventually, miners with a sore back or a bad tooth became eager for the twelve-hour, non-addictive pain relief that was being marketed to them by drug companies. Doctors were encouraged and often rewarded by manufacturers to treat every single pain complaint with pain pills.

Soon, patients of all walks of life who had taken pain pills on the advice of their doctors—pills that were strong enough to soothe post-op surgery and stage-four cancer patients—were hooked. Before long, people were crushing pills to snort, smoke or inject the drug as they fought off the withdrawal sickness when opioid levels subsided.

And yet, no alarms sounded at either the CDC or FDA even as prescriptions and refills spiraled beyond plausible numbers. Distributors simply loaded up pharmacies with more pills and collected record profits on the burgeoning sales. Records and congressional testimony from 2018 show that from 2007 to 2012, distributors sent more than 780 million hydrocodone and oxycodone pills into West Virginia: 433 pills for every man, woman and child. One town of 400 residents was sent 9 million opioid pills in two years. Another, with less than 1,800 citizens, received 16.5 million in ten years. Another, population 2,900, received almost 21 million pills during that decade.

The people who live in these mountains are primarily of Scots-Irish stock. Hardy, clannish, and distrusting of outsiders, they are nevertheless hospitable once you gain their trust. We'd made some contacts at various rehab clinics around Harlan County, Kentucky and they put us onto a man who used to deal OxyContin back in the days of the Florida pill mills and the Oxy highway, circa 2014. That was before he got a few years in prison and went through rehab. There are literally dozens of stories like his in this county alone. His stands out because he hasn't reoffended or started using again. Almost all opiate addicts eventually relapse, even when they receive the very best treatment. We pull up to his house just after sunset. There are a lot of four-wheelers and some trucks parked all around the modest shack. It's not a party; it's a hootenanny. Most everyone is outside but a fifty-something man with silver hair in his hair greets us and takes us through the house.

Like so many homes in this area, there are old appliances in the yard and on the porch, giving a first impression of derelict poverty.

But inside, the house is tidy, comfortable, and inviting. This is the character of the lowland Scots who settled Appalachia and became Americans there. These people originally came from the borderlands between England and Scotland and were the first invasion stop for English armies going back centuries. As a result, these Scots learned not to put too much of their household wealth into assets they couldn't carry away when the English invaders rolled into their territory. And they didn't put as much care into how it looked from the outside—the poorer the better in fact. A poor house was less likely to be razed and burned to the ground than one displaying outward wealth. Instead, they would invest in fast horses and mobile valuables, a legacy that played a major part in the region's history of bootlegging with pure-bred horses and later supercharged cars. Both the Kentucky Derby and NASCAR have their roots in the instincts of Appalachia's Scots-Irish settlers.

Our silver-haired host takes us to the backyard. Behind the house are about thirty people, mostly families, by the look of it. They're listening to an informal quartet playing bluegrass. There's food and plates on a table and a small bonfire, which is welcome since the night air is chilly here. And there's a still. We're told to take a log and throw it on the fire under the still. It's a customary thing. A mountain thing. Do a little work to help make the moonshine and you're one of us.

John, the former dealer and addict, saunters up and greets us with a rough handshake from an even rougher hand. He wears a slightly wary expression. The rehab clinic people contacted him and asked if he'd talk with us. He said he would, provided we don't identify him. John was a dealer and an addict, back when the shill prescription business meant you could bring in more than enough to sell while keeping as much as you wanted for personal use.

He offers us some moonshine and it lives up to the hype. There's fried chicken, greens, biscuits and more. After enough small talk to feel comfortable, and enough moonshine to make everyone friendly, John tells us how getting sent to prison was the best thing that ever happened to him.

"It wasn't just that I was gonna kill myself eventually with the pills," he says with an East Kentucky twang, "all I cared about was the high and the money I was making."

"I wasn't focused on the people besides myself I would be killing," John says. "We out here on a Saturday night doing this." He waves around the backyard at the people laughing, eating. A few have started clogging. He looks thoughtful. "How many can't cause they're dead?"

John did a stint in state prison where he first tried to use the rehab program just to get points toward early release, but through it he actually realized how bad his addiction was. He started taking it seriously. More importantly, he realized how many people's lives he'd destroyed in his own county. People he knew. Distant relatives, friends, and friends of friends. It was too much to bear without taking responsibility. It was both a figurative and a literal "come to Jesus" moment for him.

"I got out and I wasn't worried about the money no more. But I wanted to stay clean and sober." He stops and smirks sheepishly at the cup of moonshine in his hand. "Well," he says with a wink, "clean anyway." He continues, "Part of my release was continuing rehab and meetings, and I took to it better than I thought I would." He's been off the pills and everything but cigarettes, moonshine, and beer for going on four and a half years. Work comes and goes. Life is not easy out here. As of spring 2019, the unemployment rate in Harlan County is the fourth highest in the state and more than twice that of the nation as a whole. John has his share of troubles, but lack of friends and family isn't among them.

This is his home. His kin go back eight generations, at least as the family lore holds. He's got cousins and kids all over these "hollers." He's getting by, if barely, but you can tell from his eyes that he lives for nights like this. A dozen families, a fire, good food and better music. He's one of the lucky ones and you can tell it from talking to him.

"Every time I get blue over my troubles, I think about all the people right around here still hooked on that junk. And I think about them that are buried here because of it." He knows about the suicide rate and the overdose rate in Kentucky and here in Harlan. He knows he had a hand in growing it. Hard to say if it's willpower, working his program or just plain guilt that keeps him going.

We're in the right place. We'll hear dozens of stories like this before our investigation is finished. Very few of them have happy endings like John's story does. We didn't know it at the time, but we're gathering a moment of warmth and hope in a region where most hope died in recent decades.

2
The Blizzard

Starting in the 1980s, the number of opioid prescriptions in the United States began to grow, but did so slowly through the mid-1990s. Doctors were more cautious back then about the earlier kinds of painkillers because they knew they could be addictive, and pain management wasn't a priority. In the eighties and nineties, patients seeking repeated opiate prescriptions would end up blacklisted by local physicians and hospitals, who recognized them as addicts. No general physician would prescribe refillable opiates in any other than the most extreme cases. In the late 1990s, though, everything changed.

Per capita prescribing doubled year over year after that so that by the early 2010s more than 259 million prescriptions were written in the United States. That was the peak in 2013. In that year, the average prescription was for fifty-three tablets. That means in 2013 alone, there were twelve billion opioid tablets prescribed. That's enough for every single adult American to take opioids daily for five weeks. Owing to a combination of crackdowns, new guidelines, and regulations, the number of per capita opioid prescriptions has since dropped to 190 million, with each prescription now averaging only forty tablets. That's still 7.8 billion tablets being prescribed annually to a nation of 330 million people.

If a pharmacy fills two hundred prescriptions of all types on an average day, then today about twenty-five of those will be for opioids.

That's far and away the biggest single category of prescriptions filled in a pharmacy. That's in every pharmacy in America, every single day.

* * *

In very large measure, this blizzard of opioid prescriptions really started with Purdue Pharma. "Blizzard" here is not a capriciously chosen word, by the way. According to court filings, a member of the Sackler family, owners of Purdue Pharma the maker of OxyContin, told attendees of the drug's 1996 launch party that the drug's takeoff would be "followed by a blizzard of prescriptions that will bury the competition," according to filings and records produced in Massachusetts v Pursue Pharma et al. And he was right. OxyContin was the most successful pharmaceutical product launch in American history. It buried the competition in the years since. In that same period of time, OxyContin and its competitors also buried hundreds of thousands of Americans.

According to the CDC, from 1999 to 2017, more than 700,000 people died from a drug overdose. Around 68 percent of the more than 70,200 drug overdose deaths in 2017 involved an opioid. In 2017, the number of overdose deaths involving opioids was six times higher than in 1999, counting both prescription opioids and illegal opioids like heroin and illicitly manufactured fentanyl.

* * *

Experts estimate that despite the decline in opioid prescriptions, opioids could kill almost half a million Americans in the next decade, as the crisis of dependency and overdose accelerates, according to a 2017 article in *STAT News*, a journal dedicated to health, medicine and life sciences. Those seeking non-prescription relief for their dependence turn to street opioids, methamphetamines, and other substitutes, compounding the number of fatalities.

Right now, there are 130 deaths a day from opioids alone. The trail of death runs "a swath of destruction…from tiny New England suburbs to the farm country of California, from the beach towns of Florida to the Appalachian foothills," according to the article.

STAT surveyed ten leading health experts at public health universities in 2017, and the results were staggering. "In the worst-case scenario put forth by *STAT's* expert panel, that toll could spike to 250 deaths a day, if potent synthetic opioids like fentanyl and carfentanyl continue to spread rapidly and the waits for treatment continue to stretch weeks in hard-hit states like West Virginia and New Hampshire," *STAT* reports.

In the worst-case scenario, the death toll over the course of the next ten years could exceed 650,000, more than the number of Americans expected to die from breast and prostate cancer, combined.

It's hard to imagine the situation getting worse, but evidence suggests it will. And not just numerically, but on a human level. Over the course of our travels, we saw it in the individual stories of tragedy, of public overdoses, of newborns who come out of the womb already dependent on opioids.

Viral videos of people overdosing in public are now too common, like that of Ron Hiers and his wife, Carla, who shot up heroin in a Walgreens in Memphis, Tennessee and passed out at a bus stop. As *Time* described it in an article and video titled "Life after Addiction," Hiers is "bent backward over a bus-stop bench, eyes closed, head brushing the ground and a cell phone in his outstretched hand. It rings, but the man doesn't move. A few feet away, dangerously close to the road, a woman lies face down on the sidewalk, her legs buckled under her. She tries to get up but can't make it, and collapses back down in a heap."

In another heart-breaking scene, a mother lies sprawled on the floor of the toy aisle in a retail store in Lawrence, Massachusetts. Her two-year-old daughter, dressed in pink "Frozen" pajamas, cries and screams, vainly trying to wake her mother up.

Such stories, unthinkable a generation ago, can be found all across White Middle America. Flyover America. The Heartland.

A grandmother and her partner in East Liverpool, Ohio, are found sprawled out in the front seat of an idling car while her four-year-old grandson, still dressed in dinosaur pajamas, sits in the back.

Even the survival stories can make you feel a bone-deep kind of sadness. In Jacksonville, Florida, a young woman candidly told a local news station of her struggles with opioids that started when she was prescribed them at the age of sixteen to alleviate the pain of ovarian cysts. Twelve years later, she was still fighting addiction.

"I remember doing the pregnancy test, putting it on the ground and shooting up while I was waiting for the test results to come back," Crystal Harrison told First Coast News. "I was prescribed them for about two months, and when the prescription ran out I started looking in the street for them. I went from Lortab to Oxycodone to heroin to fentanyl, and all it was just, it's been a downhill effect since I was sixteen until now twenty-eight."

She's had to be revived with Narcan three times. She sought treatment, and as of the time of her interview in the fall of 2018, she had been clean for six months and regained custody of her three children. Assuming she beats the odds and stays clean, the cost in lost time with her children and to her health has already been levied, and it's all because of a drug she should have never been prescribed.

* * *

In a way, it's simple. Their first taste came from a person they trusted most—their doctor. Some might sneer at "pill poppers" for a moral failing, but the number one way Americans are introduced to prescription opioids is when they get them for acute pain for minor or major surgeries. The second most common way is wisdom tooth removal. The average age of the recipients of opioids for wisdom tooth removal is around seventeen years old.

So, we turned to a different kind of doctor for some answers: Dr. Robert Valuck, professor at the University of Colorado Denver's School of Pharmacy and Pharmaceutical Science. Valuck is a fit and gregarious man with grey peppered in his brown hair. He can hold forth on the broad scale and history of the opioid crisis, in part because he saw it unfold in real-time, but also because it's a passion he has made a part of his field of study.

And he has no qualms about naming those he considers most responsible, the merchants of this crisis. "There's a confluence of factors over a long period at play but you start in the early 1980s with the increased attention to treatment of pain and the recognition of pain," Valuck says. "There was a lot of talk about the under-treatment of pain in the 1980s and in some ways there was a little truth to that, but the narrative was completely different. No one was talking about ideas like pain-free or 'painkillers.' I don't like that word 'painkiller.' There's no such thing." Interestingly, addicts often describe opiates not as eliminating pain, but making it so they simply don't care about the pain.

While the explosion of opioid prescriptions for pain treatment and pain management began in earnest in the early 1990s, Valuck said that one of the prime movers for the push cited by pain management experts, doctors, and especially pharmaceutical companies was something printed in the January 10th, 1980 issue of the prestigious *New England Journal of Medicine*.

It wasn't a study or anything even close to so weighty. It was a single-paragraph letter to the editor. Here is the full text of it:

Addiction Rare in Patients Treated With Narcotics

To the Editor: Recently, we examined our current files to determine the incidence of narcotic addiction in 39,946 hospitalized medical patients who were monitored consecutively. Although there were 11,882 patients who received at least one narcotic preparation, there were only four cases of reasonably well documented addiction in patients who had no history of addiction. The addiction was considered major in only one instance. The drugs implicated were meperidine in two patients, Percodan in one, and hydromorphone in one. We conclude that despite widespread use of narcotic drugs in hospitals, the development of addiction is rare in medical patients with no history of addiction.

Jane Porter
Hershel Jick, MD
Boston Collaborative Drug
Surveillance Program
Boston University Medical Center

"Even now the authors admit it wasn't supposed to be carte blanche for opioids. This wasn't a real study. It was basically a larger-case anecdote," Valuck said. "This became something cited hundreds and hundreds of times as evidence for the fact that opioids were not addictive, if used legitimately. The claim was that it was less than 1 percent or one-tenth of a percent that became addicted and it showed no such thing."

The truth was, Porter and Jick had analyzed a database of patients hospitalized at Boston University Medical Center. These were patients in a hospital given small doses of opioids for acute pain, not long-term pain. The drugs were administered by staff, not the patients themselves, and were delivered only in the hospital.

But pharmaceutical companies and pain management advocates were off and running. The Joint Commission is a prestigious national non-profit that accredits and certifies nearly 21,000 health care organizations and programs in the United States. They claimed that facilities needed to create a plan for addressing levels of pain and what to do about it. This sounds reasonable in and of itself – nobody wants to live in pain.

But consider the American Pain Foundation. While also official sounding and apparently reasonable, they were anything but. Valuck describes the American Pain Foundation as "a money laundering organization for the pharmaceutical industry." Funding records bear this out. According to an investigation by ProPublica, fully 90 percent of its funding came from Big Pharma. It was the chief advocate for the proliferation of opioid pain relievers and expanded pain management as part of the medical practice for decades. That is, it was the chief advocate until it abruptly closed its doors in 2012, just as it came under intense Congressional scrutiny.

"The American Pain Foundation launched a campaign to make pain the 'fifth vital sign,'" Valuck said. The Joint Commission joined them, and in 2001 rolled out its pain management standards which supported the idea of the fifth vital sign. "They said you have to assess and address it. They were not saying you had to use opioids but to assess and address it," Valuck said. "That set the foundation."

That may sound benign to a layman but think about it. What are the four things you get checked every time you go to see your doctor? It's always body temperature, pulse rate, respiration rate, and blood pressure.

"Now, every person at every visit to the doctor would get assessed and asked about it," Valuck said. "It would put the issue top of mind, and plant the idea that any pain they had should be treated. But pain is not a vital sign. It is a symptom."

So, taking together all of this, Valuck said, you had a generation of doctors taught to think of pain as a "vital sign" and that any and all pain had to be managed or ameliorated. It created a culture where doctors and patients alike viewed pain not as part of the human experience, or a natural warning sign, or even as a consequence, but rather as something that had to be eradicated.

Concurrent with the rise of the concept in medicine of perpetual pain management and eradication came the inclusion of pain management as part of the patient experience with government payment plans. "Then there were discharge surveys for Medicare and Medicaid patients. Satisfaction surveys of care. Now granted... only a random sample of patients get these... but they were asked about how their pain was managed," Valuck said. "And until only recently, scores on the pain segment were tied to higher and lower levels of reimbursement for the provider. I can't think of a more perverse incentive for hospitals and providers to overprescribe.

"It created a perverse incentive to give everyone Vicodin. 'Are you in pain? Have some Vicodin,'" Valuck said, mimicking the dismissive attitude.

But was it just misguided medical policies and a simple push from Big Pharma that got us here? "Don't underestimate the power of marketing... the pharmaceutical companies never did," Valuck said.

* * *

Big Pharma first marketed prescription opioids such as hydrocodone to treat pain. They claimed, leaning on the conventional wisdom of the Porter-Jick letter and what came after, that these drugs carried minimal risk for addiction. There are dozens of companies that manufacture and market opioids and synthetic opioids, but the biggest name in the business, especially when it comes to marketing, is Purdue Pharma run by the Sackler family.

Mortimer Sackler was the patriarch of the Sackler dynasty until his death in 2010. The second son of Jewish immigrants from Ukraine and Poland, Sackler and his three brothers became the leaders of a small pharmaceutical company in the 1950s. By the mid-1980s, Purdue Pharma was still a small concern, but Mortimer Sackler had big ideas on how to grow its product line.

"Mr. Sackler... is associated with a lot of well-known products like Valium and Librium, but he invented peer-to-peer influencing, thought leader influencing, and how to get doctors to sell to each other," Valuck said.

That is to say, rather than relying on the typical "cute sales rep" that would go from doctor's office to doctor's office, Purdue spent tens of millions on programs to convince physicians to lean on one another to favor certain Purdue products over other pharmaceutical brands. Doctors, most of whom hold themselves in high esteem, naturally hold their peers and their peers' recommendations in high esteem.

Purdue Pharma was a pioneer in campaigns geared towards patients directly, such as the "Get Your Life Back" campaign that was basically preparing the market for Purdue and the Sackler's greatest achievement—the launch of OxyContin in 1996.

It all worked all too well.

"OxyContin was the most successful launch in the history of modern medicine," Valuck says. By 2001, something like 80 percent of Purdue's gross revenue of $3 billion came from OxyContin sales. And according to the *New Yorker*, OxyContin had generated for Purdue "some $35 billion in revenue" by 2017. The Sackler family had gone from owners of a relatively modest pharmaceutical company in the mid-1980s to the nineteenth wealthiest family in America in 2016, according to *Forbes*.

Pharmaceutical companies like Purdue and others continued the full-court press. Strategies included paying middlemen to get around state regulations and even going so far as to allegedly bribe doctors to prescribe opioid medications.

"They knew what was going on. They knew [OxyContin] was more addictive than they let on. They knew it wasn't a twelve-hour medication. And it will eventually get proven in court," Valuck said. "They've already paid multiple hundred-million-dollar judgments—they've already admitted that [it] doesn't last as long as they claimed."

More than forty states are involved in a multi-district litigation in Ohio. Hundreds of counties and municipalities have their own lawsuits. Whether Purdue survives or not is in the cards, but the damage to Americans has already been done. If the tobacco company lawsuits are any guide, little of the settlement money will end up in the pockets of victims. More likely, it ends up in government hands, which will then distribute it to corporate recovery programs with maddeningly ineffective recovery statistics. Either way, the price will be paid by Middle America.

Some media attention has been paid to the incredible body count the opioid epidemic has wrought, but there has been very little sense of emergency, and no sense of urgency. Not the way there was with the crack epidemic of the 1980s. Particularly not at the level of national policy and national media.

At the state level, some of the regions hardest hit have cracked down on "pill mills" where unscrupulous doctors took cash for prescriptions in storefronts that would pop up and disappear from month to month. And they've passed limits on the amount or duration of opioids physicians can prescribe. Of course, as mentioned before, this has only resulted in a grim game of drug choice "Whack a Mole" with those enthralled to opioid dependence seeking illicit sources like heroin and fentanyl.

The addictive nature of opioids has been known for over a century. Today, it isn't simply anecdotal. We can almost measure the likelihood of addiction to the tablet. According to Valuck, there is a 6 percent chance a person given just 6 tablets will be taking opioids a year later. This comes from a survey of over half a million patients, not a letter to the editor of a medical journal. "And if you give a patient three weeks or more of tablets, say 60-90, there is a 20 percent chance they'll be taking opioids a year later. Give them forty days— it's a 40 percent chance. We know how this works," he said. The calculus of opiate addiction is as consistent as it is depressing.

* * *

Many states have passed regulations limiting opioid prescriptions, and medical guidelines increasingly stress that opioids be avoided when possible for acute pain such as a new injury, or for patients who are post-op. There are new systems in various states where prescribers can look up a patient's entire prescription history with other prescribers to ensure that the patient isn't "doctor shopping."

But there's still the problem of illicit opioids, synthetics, and the persistent problem of those who have taken opioids for chronic, long-term issues.

"The most reduction has been in acute pain, but we've not gotten our hands on chronic pain, those who are physiologically dependent," Valuck said. "There's no real data to support opioids as long-term pain relief, and yet there are data emerging that people on opioids for longer periods are developing hyperalgesia,"—which is characterized by a patient receiving opioids potentially becoming, paradoxically, more sensitive to pain.

"These people aren't addicts but they are physiologically dependent. In these cases, we're really not treating pain but treating withdrawal. And they are teetering on the edge of addiction. It just robs the spirit and it robs a person of purpose," he said. "Anyone can be tapered off but it takes time and commitment," Valuck added. "That's the next big challenge."

* * *

If we were investigating a crime, a murder, then what we have established so far is the means. We still need to dig into the motive, and more importantly, we need to look at the body. So, we turned south from Kentucky to Alabama. Another small town. Another old coal town. Another working class town. Another victim of this crime.

3
A Town as a Corpse

Jasper, Alabama is a rural town of just 14,000 residents located in the northwest part of the state. It has the sort of tree-lined, shady streets that characterize so much of small town America. It's also a hotspot for prescription opiate abuse. Jasper has the highest death by overdose rate in the state and the fifth highest in the nation.

Downtown Jasper is probably not what you think about when you picture a small town in the Deep South. Sure, there's the archetypal Southern courthouse surrounded by a well-manicured lawn complete with monuments to Civil War heroes and town founders. There are the old two-story buildings across the street, home to various law firms whose names read like the membership roster at the Kappa Alpha Order. That part of Jasper is right out of a John Grisham novel.

Right off the main street, there's the much-lauded Twisted Barley Brewery bar and grill, alongside the very trendy New American joint Warehouse 319. There's a yoga studio, a hand-crafted ice cream parlor, an upscale tobacconist called the Cigar Box, and a hip sushi joint. A stylish coffee house recently featured on one of those network TV hidden camera reality shows. It feels less Old South and more New Urban mixed use.

It was a surprising find in this sleepy little town northwest of Birmingham. But leave the confines of the downtown, and along the main highway that cuts through Jasper you find your standard dollar stores, chain restaurants, big box stores, and so on. Go a few blocks west of downtown and you find yourself among lower-end housing and then housing that barely qualifies as such—shacks with no electricity or water and mobile homes with boarded windows. This part of Jasper feels like an American favela, where poverty and abundance live within mere blocks of one another.

Look a little closer and you begin to notice the number of boarded up storefronts in areas just a few blocks away from the downtown. There's a proliferation of payday lenders, bail bondsmen and pawn shops, and a surprising number of treatment centers and rehabilitation clinics. Most focus on opioid and meth dependence. It's a town of stark contrasts.

Alabama has the highest opioid prescription rate per capita as of 2018, according to the US Centers for Disease Control and Prevention. And Jasper, it turns out, is at the epicenter of the opioid crisis. Jasper is the county seat of Walker County, which has the highest prescription rate per patient in Alabama, and the highest overdose death rate.

Just before Christmas in 2016, Walker County saw eighteen overdoses reported in a single day, and twenty-two over a three-day period. Three of the victims died. In one of the cases, two individuals traveling in a vehicle with a three-year-old overdosed at the same time and crashed, according to local newspaper reports. The number of overdoses in Walker County is staggering. As of 2018, the annual drug death rate per one hundred thousand residents was listed at 47.5 for Walker County, compared to 16.0 for all of Alabama. As of 2017, the opioid prescription rate for Walker County was 216.1 prescriptions per one hundred residents. That's more than two prescriptions for every single resident of the county.

We spent a week in Jasper, talking to law enforcement, treatment experts, community leaders, and ordinary people. We went to local restaurants, coffee houses, bars, laundry mats, and other venues. Every single person we talked to knew someone close who had overdosed, not merely someone with an opioid dependency problem.

Most everyone in America knows someone who has struggled with this demon. They knew someone close who had overdosed, and too many knew someone close who had overdosed and died.

* * *

Most people don't associate Alabama with coal mining, but Jasper was once among the leading producers of coal. That's part of the reason why there's such a gap between the rich and poor here. It's also why the area suffers problems similar to better-known coal areas like the towns in Kentucky and West Virginia. At its height there were half a dozen coal mines, two sandstone quarries, four hundred coke ovens and a foundry, according to the *Daily Mountain Eagle*.

Mining and its associated trades are hard, repetitive work that easily give injuries to the common workers, while making large profits for the owners. These injured workers were a natural target for pharmaceutical companies going back to the 1980s, when they began pushing for more aggressive treatment of pain.

"Physicians were prescribing it like crazy," said Matt Brown, chief of staff at Addiction Recovery Care in Louisa, Kentucky. "We're from coal country. It's a lot of manual labor and a lot of injuries. And when the coal jobs go away, people still have their prescriptions. They have a dependence on the drug and a need to make money on the side."

Government subsidies helped fuel Jasper's addiction. As coal jobs started disappearing, Medicare and Medicaid ensured that retired or unemployed patients would still be able to get their medications. Moreover, the price of opioid tablets on the street was high enough in recent decades that many could sell pills to others while still having enough left to satisfy their dependence, perversely replacing some of the income lost to globalization. Ironically, patient health may have been at greater risk by having health insurance, Medicare, or Medicaid than not having it, due to the lack of interest the government showed in how it was being used and affecting people's lives.

Judge Henry P. Allred has seen the crisis unfold, up close, for years now. He is the district judge for the Fourteenth Judicial Circuit of Alabama and head of Walker County's drug court, which is an alternative program combining criminal justice with drug rehabilitation programs. Allred's court tries to break the revolving door between drug dependence and punishment in the judicial system.

Allred is young for the bench, just forty-three at the time of this writing, with a full, peppery beard and the kind of stylish, slightly longer hair you associate with young Southern lawyers and seersucker suits. He reminds us of Matthew McConaughey in *A Time to Kill*. A graduate of the University of Alabama, he has a deep, thick Southern accent and pronounces "them" with two syllables. He's been on the bench since 2009 and in charge of the drug court since 2013, the very height of the prescription opioid blizzard. We sat down to talk to him in his modest office in the court annex, which is adorned with pictures of his two young daughters and Roll Tide memorabilia.

"Back as recently as 2016, I would say 80-85 percent of opioid cases we saw dealt with prescription opioids. Now, today, it's at least 80 percent heroin," Allred says. "Heroin made a big comeback when law enforcement took care of the pill mills. With heroin there's no quality control and you don't know what you're getting. I think that's what's behind the overdoses."

While it may be true that the worst of the pill mills in Walker County were closed down, Walker County still leads the state in the rate of prescribed opioids as recently as 2018. Allred thinks it's a case of the waters being shallow but wide. Prescribers are staying within newer guidelines but still writing prescriptions generously.

"Well, our physicians here in Walker County are wonderful, and after the pill mills were shut down, there was still a demand. And if you're going to be a prescriber, you're going to have to treat people who want some kind of opioids, or they'll just go somewhere else."

His title may be judge, but he comes across as more an advocate trying to help the people who end up in front of his bench. "I think this is a symptom of a larger decline in society. We've always had pain pills here—this is coal country. With the coal jobs going away, though, you see the parents, and then their children and then their grandchildren get caught up in this cycle," Allred says. "You have grandparents having to raise grandchildren because their parents are off in jail or dead, and then the grandparents die and there's no one left to take care of the kids. What do you think will happen with a lot of those kids?"

"We have generations now of people raised on disability and never knowing anything more," he says, "And it takes over their lives."

He tells the story of one young man, twenty-four and a father, he had in his court who was trying to get back to a relationship with his daughter. As part of the drug court program, his activities and visitation were closely monitored. The young man was on disability, had a legal prescription for an opioid painkiller, and was tested regularly to ensure he wasn't abusing.

"Then I noticed he would regularly miss his visitation with his daughter, but he would not miss a single doctor's visit to get his 120 Lortab 10 mgs every month," Allred says. "You see the kind of priorities this addiction creates."

Allred says it has robbed people of any ambition or sense of purpose, which is as insidious as the addiction itself. "We have a component of people who come through here and the best they can imagine for their life is getting on disability and getting that $700 a month check. That's all they look forward to and all they know. It's what their parents knew. They live with their girlfriend's mother or in some other situation and they just want barely enough to get by on and to get their prescriptions."

With that, they can self-medicate and sell any extras for quite the markup to more well-heeled opioid seekers. And while the pill mills may largely be gone, it is not that difficult nor is it illegal to get refillable, ongoing prescriptions for chronic pain. Prescriptions that often come in very large quantities.

* * *

We stopped by a standalone clinic off Highway 78. It looks a little run down and advertises in big letters on faded red trim that it offers internal medicine and primary care, as well as treatment for neurology pain and headaches.

Inside, we asked the receptionist what it would take to see the doctor if we were from out of state and had no insurance. The price would be $300 up front, and we would have to provide referrals and charts from a primary care physician. After that, treatment for chronic pain would be $200 a month. That treatment would allow us to obtain and maintain an ongoing prescription for opiates.

We have no reason to think the doctor at this clinic, Samia S. Moizuddin, MD, would deviate in any way from medical practices or state restrictions on opioid prescriptions. But the cost of getting opioid prescriptions remains exceptionally low, assuming a patient presents with the symptoms required to justify such treatment in the eyes of regulators and the law.

According to ProPublica's Prescriber Checkup database, in 2016, the last year for which data is available, Moizuddin had 10,707 Medicare prescriptions filled, nearly thirty a day. Eighty percent of her patients were low income. Gabapentin was her most frequently prescribed medication. It's a non-opioid antiepileptic and nerve pain reliever. It is followed immediately by hydrocodone-acetaminophen, which was prescribed to 42 percent of her patients. Oxycodone HCL, oxycodone- acetaminophen, and methadone HCL were other opioids in her top ten most common and frequent prescriptions.

Taken together, and using data from Medicare's 2016 prescription-drug program as listed on ProPublica, fully 92.6 percent of Moizuddin's patients appear to receive some form of opioid prescriptions. This compares to Moizzudin's peers, for whom just 23.5 percent of their patients receive some kind of opioid prescription.

Moizuddin's repeated use of Gabapentin may be especially dangerous, as nearly a quarter of addicts attending recovery programs have a history of abusing Gabapentin. It is particularly common among opiate users, because Gabapentin appears to enhance the euphoria associated with opiate use, creating a particularly addictive cocktail. Both Kentucky and Michigan have recently upgraded Gabapentin's regulatory status, classifying it as a Schedule V controlled substance.

Opioids are simply not very difficult or expensive to obtain legally, despite the state's efforts to impose additional rules on their distribution. The most frequent prescribers in Alabama are all over the state. It's just that it's the residents of Walker County who are getting the prescriptions, whether in the county or elsewhere.

Allred has seen people come before him looking like they have every chance at getting cleaned up and their life back together, but too often it doesn't work that way. He has pages of heart-breaking stories where he's done everything he can for someone and he still gets word weeks or months later that they're back in jail or dead. He's seen people who actually get cleaned up do so too late and end up having severe medical problems from the damage they've already done to their heart or liver.

"You shouldn't be thirty-three or thirty-four and having to deal with open heart surgery or liver failure," Allred tells us. "The saddest thing for me though is seeing younger people, millennials, coming through here, and I can see exactly what's coming for them and they don't get it."

He pauses for a moment and shakes his head. "Everything we do seems like it's one step forward and two steps back," Allred says. That's not to say there hasn't been progress, but Jasper has the same problem we observed in Kentucky. Even as they crack down on pill mills, heroin and Fentanyl slide right in to fill the gap."

* * *

Sheriff Nick Smith has seen the problem from both the point of view of a drug warrior and, now, as something more. Smith is a striking figure. Clean cut, blonde, blue eyed, and fit, he's the archetypal All-American boy grown up. Still in his early 30s, this father of four has been both the youngest police chief and now the youngest sheriff in the history of the state of Alabama.

Coming out of the academy, he was a hard charger. He was all about the numbers and the arrests. He put together an arrest record that took him from recruit in Parrish, Alabama to police chief in Cordova by the age of twenty-one. In January 2019, he took office as Walker County Sheriff.

"I thought I was making a difference. We were busting people in the most drug infested town in Alabama—back then it was crack, coke and meth—and I thought I was being tough on crime," Smith says. He doesn't mention it while we're in his office, preferring to maintain a friendly poker face, but as we speak his deputies are cooperating with local police on a massive warrant roundup. He's going after the dealers, not the folks with simple possession warrants. The local paper on Saturday will announce more than forty arrests.

"But after a while I realized I was arresting the same people over and over for possession," Smith says. "And then after a few more years I was arresting their children. Or their grandchildren."

He recalls one person who changed his outlook. It was a young woman. He'd arrested her about four times in one month on opioid possession charges. She was released to a rehab program but never showed up. Another day, another warrant. But this one got to Smith.

"I spent two weeks hunting her up. She ran even though she had a daughter dying of leukemia. When we found her, she told me 'I ain't always been like this—my four-year-old is dying,'" he recounts, then turns reflective. "I've got four children and I'd like to think in the same circumstances I wouldn't turn to alcohol or drugs, but if that's all it takes for someone…" he says, the sentence going unfinished.

A cloud passes over his face, "I saw her about a year later. She'd gotten cleaned up and had a job, and we'd gotten her released early," Smith says. "Then her daughter died. Now she's a missing person case. I don't know what happened to her."

Smith has tried to be innovative, too. A colleague told him about a program in Mississippi called Project Mercy and he started his own local version in Walker County. It allows people with or without warrants to come to the police station and ask for help with their drug or alcohol problems. No charges, no mess. Existing charges would have to be worked out, but the focus was on getting people help without the fear of additional criminal repercussions. He also initiated programs for existing inmates to get them more help beyond simply getting sober.

"A lot of people in jail aren't bad once you get the drugs out of their system. But then they get out and they end up back with the same people, or facing fines they can't pay, or not being able to get a job because they have a record or no driver's license—and they end up going right back to their habits," Smith says. "They try to get things back together and they have old fines or whatever and they can't get out of the cycle. They don't have any chance to get back on a good path."

Then Smith says something you don't often hear from young law enforcement officers, much less your typical small-town sheriff. "That's the thing about the criminal justice system—once you get in the system, the system won't let you go. You're generating revenue," Smith says.

While police chief in Cordoba, the town saw an 80 percent reduction in crime. Smith says it's not all because of the comprehensive approach he took to law enforcement and drug crimes. But it's clear his approach had substantial impact there.

"We have to provide a better way for people caught up in this.

There's not a family in this county, rich or poor, who isn't affected by this. I got it in my family just like everyone else," Smith says. "We need more programs to help the addicts instead of filling the jails with addicts. You're spending the money either way, may as well get people help."

His voice gets a hard edge to it and suddenly he is every bit the Southern Sheriff. "We have to focus on the people selling and profiting. That's the people we have to go after." His jaw muscles tighten. "Both the merchants of street drugs and pharmaceuticals."

* * *

A few days later we're at dinner with Jennifer Smith, the second-term city councilwoman for district four, which contains some of the poorer neighborhoods west of downtown Jasper. She's no relation to Sheriff Smith.

Smith is a fit, blonde widow in her forties and is old school Walker County. Her father and grandfather worked in the county coal mines. Smith worked for years for the city as director of the recreation program, and is no babe in the woods when it comes to drug use in the area.

Everyone knew about meth going back to the 2000s and about opioid pills. She first learned about heroin in Walker County being a problem, though, when her twenty-three-year-old niece, Maggie Williams Thornell, wife and mother of one, died of a heroin overdose in the summer of 2015. "In some of the areas I represent it's generational. It's a cycle like you see in inner cities," Smith says. "And then it is a problem that we get people through rehab and clean, and they still have outstanding fines holding them back."

Smith fights an uphill battle, she says, trying to convince other city council members and community leaders about how some kind of amnesty work program might help former addicts get their lives on track. People from the more monied families haven't been immune to the opioid scourge, but they aren't as aware of the costs. With a wide gap between rich and poor and a smaller than usual middle class in Jasper, that only steepens the hill she's climbing.

Among Smith's ideas is that instead of having to pay old fines and fees, people who qualify could work them off through community service. "The people I'm trying to convince don't understand how an extra twenty-five or fifty dollars a week could make a difference between feeding the kids and paying the light bill. And if you're in that kind of misery, what's to stop you from wanting to medicate yourself?" Smith asks. "I know amnesty is a buzzword, but we're not talking about letting people off scot free, but letting them work it off."

* * *

The troubles for Jasper and Walker County run deep, and the opioid epidemic touches almost every aspect of those troubles. Not long after President Trump's election, the coal industry received a welcome boost in the form of increased tariffs on cheap foreign coal. A coal company began looking at reopening operations in one of the Walker County mines. They wanted to create 250 new jobs in Jasper for people working in mining operations.

Coal mining jobs are hard work but they pay very well. There are ancillary jobs in support of coal mining, as well. Commercial driving, engineering, supply, logistics and other secondary services would be in greater demand as the result of the new mining activity. It was an exciting time for the area. It didn't last.

The company started drug testing potential hires. They couldn't find enough workers who could pass. "They discovered we didn't have 250 workers who could pass," Judge Allred says. "Only one in four people who tested passed the drug test." Some new industries, even some high-tech businesses, have opened shop in Walker County, but none with the scale of high-paying jobs well-suited to the working class people in the area.

Opioids hadn't just killed people in this town. Opioids killed this town.

* * *

Matt Tucker is a former medical doctor whose wife committed suicide last year after years of battling addiction and mental illness. Tucker and his late wife were both addicts and alcoholics. They met in the early 2000s in rehab. The next decade and a half would see them both battling addictions, with periods of sobriety punctuated by the birth of a daughter.

Tucker is a stocky guy with a shaven head, an unshaven face and a perpetual light in his eyes. The light has a bittersweet source; it comes from a year of living completely sober and having given up his life to God after he came home to find that his wife had hanged herself in their daughter's bedroom. Their daughter was with grandparents.

We're at Lavish Coffee with Tucker. The coffee house is almost too hip and is right across from the Jasper Civic Center. Tucker was already a functional alcoholic at nineteen with a liver that was going bad. His father, a Baptist preacher, got him into a program where he met an older psychiatrist. Tucker got clean and worked his AA program, and surprised himself and those around him by getting into the College of Medicine at the University of South Alabama in Mobile.

"Then I met a girl," Tucker says, "which is how every one of my relapse stories begins." After a few dates his first year in medical school, he started drinking again and taking opiates. He drank his way through medical school, which shows how much wasted potential the man had. So many people can't get through medical school sober. He did it drunk.

After medical school he got a surgical residency and really started in on the pills. He got caught, got himself into rehab again, and that's where he met a girl again. Her name was Dalana, a straight-A student and an exceptional athlete at both Carbon Hill High School in Alabama and the University of Southern Mississippi. She earned a bachelor's degree in nursing and became the charge nurse at UAB's Bone Marrow Transplant Unit.

They got married after getting out of rehab on the same day. He took a research job. He kept his license but didn't practice. They had a daughter, but during the pregnancy Dalana was discovered to have stage 4 metastatic breast cancer. The stresses were incredible on both of them. It wasn't long until they were getting high together.

They moved to Walker County around 2008. By that time, they had progressed to injecting fentanyl. Care for their daughter fell to their in-laws who lived down the street. Tucker and his wife were high every night. They would take so much fentanyl, it became regular for them to perform CPR on one another.

"Some addicts will tell you the chance that they could die when they shoot up is the ultimate high," Tucker says. They tried hard to get clean, but could only manage to interlace periods of sobriety and using. Their in-laws largely raised their daughter. During one period of sobriety, Dalana underwent a psychotic break. Tucker blames it on their extensive drug use.

Tucker had been clean for months leading up to Dalana's suicide. Sitting in the house while the police inspected the scene, his wife's cold body next to him, Tucker says that's when he really spoke to God. "In the middle of this dark moment I realized I was still trying to control things, even when talking to God. That's when I surrendered, and it was like a fire lit inside of me. He told me that this was not going to be in vain. I could use this to help others. That Dalana and I could help others."

In March 2018, Tucker became a patient care educator at Capstone Rural Health Center, where his job is to improve how Walker County helps those seeking recovery. He also started a daily Opiates Anonymous program at Desperation Church, which is held at the Jasper Civic Center. It's usually a full house. Before that, the only

Twelve Step group in the town met monthly. He also teaches classes at the Walker County Jail for nonviolent drug offenders who are seeking recovery.

And he rebuilt his relationship with his daughter. "This is where God wants me and where I can make a difference," Tucker says and smiles.

* * *

It often seems like the only people who really understand the opioid crisis and its impact on the community in Walker County are those either dealing with it from within the criminal justice system or those who have themselves been in thrall to opioids.

Kristen Shaw is another one of the latter. She's an attractive woman of thirty-six years with fresh highlights and manicured nails. It's a cold February day so she's in a clingy yellow sweater with a cross around her neck. For five years she's been the executive director of Hope for Women, a program in Jasper that offers a one-year in-patient program for women trying to beat the cycle of addiction and rebuild their lives.

She looks like a grown-up sorority girl. She's actually an ex-con.

Shaw was seventeen when she started smoking marijuana and taking opioid pills with her mother and step-father. In fact, opioids were pretty much the family business. Back in the late 1990's, she and her family members would practice how to fake injuries and what to say to doctors to get pain medication prescriptions. They would load up in the car and go to several medical clinics in a day. They'd get enough for their personal use, while also acquiring an inventory of pills for resale. They pulled in thousands a month from dealing their illicitly obtained prescriptions.

"We were spiraling out of control," Shaw says. At twenty-three, she met someone who promised to help her get off opioids. But his solution was to get her high on the meth he was cooking. Within a year she was facing a possible life sentence for conspiracy to commit murder and robbery in the first degree, charges arising from her relationship with her meth-cooking white knight. She plead down to felony assault and got six years in state prison, of which she had to serve two-and-a-half years.

While in prison she got her GED and graduated from a tech school where she learned to drive a forklift. She obtained a variety of certifications for sobriety and had every intention of staying clean when she got out.

"When I left prison, my mom picked me up. That's when I knew there was no hope for me. She stopped on the way home to sell a hundred methadone pills to someone. That night I relapsed," Shaw says. "I hated it but it was my life. I ended up with third degree burns on my leg from a fire in a meth lab. I ended up buying and selling and taking pills. My mom was OD'ing once a month."

Three years later, she had enough. She can't tell you any particular reason why, but one night Shaw took every drug she had, built a fire outside and burned them. Then, she called her old Sunday school teacher from her youth and asked for help. The teacher got Shaw in a program.

Shaw went through the Hope for Women program in another town and a year later she became a staffer. Shortly after that, on May 24th, 2013, her mother died of an overdose. It was just two days after Shaw's birthday and as good a day as any to mark the height of the prescription drug crisis in America.

Shaw got married to someone she met in rehab. He struggled with his sobriety and they ended up getting divorced. He died of an overdose in the fall of 2018. Just three years ago the father of her children, another man, died of a heroin overdose. Shaw counts herself lucky to have gotten out alive.

In 2014 she took over as director of the Jasper Hope for Women program. Her program accepts twenty-four women a year. Attendees start with highly monitored living, followed by a slow reintegration into society. They work on job-related skills, save money, and become mentors for newer girls in the program. They eventually graduate, but maintain a lifeline open to the program after, helping to ensure that they don't relapse.

It's been highly successful—Shaw herself is a great example—but it's both time consuming and costly to operate the program. "A lot of the county has opened up to seeing this as the epidemic it is and they've pitched in to support us, but we are only helping a handful at a time," Shaw says.

This reminds us of something Judge Allred said. "We're not going to arrest our way out of this. This isn't just a crime problem. It's a medical addiction problem." Sheriff Smith observed that we're going to be spending money on these people whether we put them in jail or put them through programs. But no program in the world can help an addict or drug dependent person who doesn't want help.

There are no easy answers. But in Jasper, Alabama, a focal point of the prescription opioid epidemic, there are a lot of good people working on trying to figure it out. They have to. Death by overdose is a specter haunting their every day.

And the death here is not just about the overdoses, tragic as they may be. There's a death of the spirit. And because so many are putting so much energy in trying to figure out a way to beat back this opioid plague, whether it's by healing the sick or arresting the guilty or rebuilding shattered lives, we think of the opportunity cost to Jasper of this battle they're fighting.

This is a small town doing its level-best to be a nice place to live. What if all the money, resources, and time spent on the anti-opioid crusade could have been spent on making more of the whole of the city like the quaint downtown? What if 250 coal jobs had returned to Jasper? What if the next generation of Jasper's youth wasn't haunted by the despair caused by their parents' addictions?

What if? Those are two of the most tragic words in the English language. It may as well be Jasper's city motto.

4
The Rot

This isn't just the story of the destruction of one town's potential. When opiates burn a community, the ashes spawn a maelstrom of crime and despair. Theft. Robbery. Prostitution. Child abuse. Domestic violence. Gang violence. Murder. The opioid crisis we're investigating spreads like a cancer, and it reacts to any attempt to prune it like the mythological Hydra. When one head is cut off, two more grow back.

Eastern Kentucky is home to people who can still trace their roots back to before the American Revolution. Here among the rolling hills and low mountains of Appalachia, strangers are rare and kin are rarely far.

We're at Crisp's Dairy Treat on Route 716 in Ashland. It's a drive-through established in 1960 that specializes in ice cream, hot dogs, onion rings and burgers. They make their burgers in a way that fast-food chains will never understand. The place has been a family venture since day one.

We're having ice cream with Rhonda Hardin on a bench outside. She's a forty-something fairy of a woman, just over five foot, and her personality runs hot and cold. Her laugh is infectious, but her sense of humor can be dark. When she gets angry, full-grown men snap to.

There's a reason behind her passion. She's buried almost a dozen family members who died from opioid abuse. "This is a plague. That's the only word for it," Hardin tells us. She's got short dark hair and an olive complexion, but she's of old Scots-Irish stock like everyone around here. Family trees in this part of the country are more like family forests—people here treat their first and second cousins like brothers and sisters and they know extended family in way that urban Americans just don't anymore.

We're talking about her unsuccessful 2018 run for city commissioner when a Crisp's employee comes outside for a smoke break. The younger woman compliments Hardin's yellow and black striped Camaro. Within minutes they're talking about mutual friends from school and from around the small towns in these hollers, despite their twenty-year difference. Their families know each other. It's not a bit surprising.

This is a place where the people are tied to the soil and the hills. Hardin tells us stories of her extended family and its history, which is etched into the rock around us. She tells us about the generations of veterans who served in America's military, and the men who worked the steel mills, and the deep mines digging coal. It's a bittersweet melding of pride and sorrow.

Then she tells us of the pills and the heroin and the crime that have followed, and the people who got rich off of it. She tells of the rot opioids have brought. "There's basically a war against my people here. Not a war, a slaughter. They're destroying entire generations to make their blood money," she says. "People are dying and killing themselves. They're not having children. These are the people who are always first to volunteer when their country calls them to war."

"But now their country turns their backs on us. Meanwhile, they just brought in thousands of people from Syria and set them up in West Virginia with homes, schools and money. But they won't help the people right here. Our people," Hardin says bitterly. "People aren't replaceable. We won't have American values without Americans. They want to replace us."

* * *

This is steel and coal country. When both industries started dying so did the people here. But in the despair that followed, one industry flourished—crime.

We're in the Tri-State Area where Ohio, Kentucky, and West Virginia come together along the Big Sandy and Ohio Rivers. The Big Sandy meanders northward from the Appalachian Mountains of Eastern Virginia along a twenty-nine-mile course that terminates at the Ohio River. Big Sandy forms a portion of the border between West Virginia and Kentucky and the Ohio River forms their Northern borders with that state.

A few miles east of where the Big Sandy flows into the Ohio River is the Port of Huntington Tri-State, the busiest inland port in the United States. It sees some sixty million tons of cargo move through annually.

This area is home to more than 360,000 people spread across the three states. It's a very homogenous place, where Whites make up more than 95 percent of the metropolitan area's population. But it's one of the nation's poorest places, too. The area has a median household income of just $30,000, which is less than half the national average. Almost to a family, the local people are Scots-Irish with some admixture. Some families trace their roots back to the initial pioneers. Many have not moved more than a hundred miles from where their ancestors settled in the middle of the eighteenth century.

Huntington, West Virginia is the largest single town in the area, with a population of almost 48,000. Huntington is also the murder capital of West Virginia, both in terms of the murder rate and the total number of homicides. Folks within a few hundred miles often refer to it as "Little Detroit." According to the most recent FBI crime statistics, Huntington's murder rate was 33.4 per 100,000 in 2017. Detroit itself saw a murder rate of 39.6 in 2017. The US national rate in that year was a mere 5.3 per 100,000 people, or about one-sixth of Huntington's rate.

Huntington is ground zero for organized criminal groups that bring pills and heroin into this part of the country. It's a destination for traffickers and dealers, and there's lots of profit to be had following the shutdown of the Florida pill mill pipeline.

Detroit isn't the only source, but it's by far the biggest. At first it was just that the product was brought into Huntington from Detroit, but increasingly dealers from Detroit set up permanent shop in the city. Locals call them the "D Boys." From Huntington the drugs would flow out into the surrounding hills and hollers, where officials think as much as 20 percent of the population are active opioid addicts.

Detroit remains the biggest source of drugs and crime and its dealers are the most embedded, according to Huntington Police Chief Hank Dial. But a new source comes from closer to home, he says. Dial says Akron, Ohio is now the primary source city for Huntington's fentanyl and carfentanyl supply.

Dial tells of one Akron-Huntington case dating back to August 2016. On a single day in that late summer, there were twenty-eight overdoses within a five-hour span. Two died, but the rest were revived with Narcan. "Our resources were stretched near their breaking point," Dial says. Bruce Griggs of Akron was arrested for the supply that nearly killed thirty people. Griggs was sentenced in 2017 in federal court to 220 months in prison with three years of supervised release.

If the cost in terms of crime in this area is staggering, then the cost in terms of overdose deaths is even more so. In a nation overcome with a widespread crisis of opiate addiction, West Virginia, which is ranked thirty-eighth in population and forty-eighth in income, is number one in overdose fatalities per capita. The rate there is 57.8 per 100,000, according to data from the US Centers for Disease Control and Prevention. It's held the top spot for years. Ohio is ranked second at 46.3 deaths by overdose per 100,000. Kentucky's rate was 37.2.

West Virginia also leads the nation in raw economic costs associated with the opioid crisis and its accompanying death and crime. According to a 2018 study by the American Enterprise

Institute, West Virginia spends $8.8 billion a year, or 12 percent of the state's gross domestic product, dealing with opiates in one way or another. In order to estimate the overall economic burden of fatal overdoses, the study considered each state's spending on health care, substance abuse rehabilitation and treatment, and criminal justice and it projected lost worker productivity.

Rahul Gupta, West Virginia's public health commissioner, has made multiple public statements that the opioid crisis is costing the state upwards of 1/8th of its economy, almost $9 billion a year, in a state that can't afford it. West Virginia is the only state losing a double-digit percentage of its economy to the opioid crisis. In a state with an annual budget of less than $5 billion, an American Enterprise Institute study places the annual cost here at nearly $4,800 per resident. That's 40 percent more than second-ranked Maryland, which spends nearly $3,400 per resident. But that's only about 5.4 percent of Maryland's GDP and less than half the relative impact suffered by West Virginia. In Ohio the cost is $2,800 per resident, and in Kentucky, it's $2,270.

* * *

In early 2019, the Drug Enforcement Administration landed in Celina, Tennessee. Locals pronounce it "se-LINE-uh," and it's just a little west and south of Huntington. They took action against two locally owned pharmacies that were dealing opioid pills in insane amounts. Celina has just 1,400 residents, but four independent and one chain pharmacy.

Two of those pharmacies combined to fill prescriptions for an eye-popping 2.5 million opioid pills in 2018, years after most states had started more closely monitoring prescriptions and limiting how much and how often doctors could prescribe opioids.

This trafficking of opiates through otherwise legal pharmacies became such an obvious criminal racket that the US Drug

Enforcement Administration and the US Department of Justice took unprecedented action. In an unprecedented injunction, the federal government ordered these pharmacies, the owner, and three different pharmacists from dispensing any controlled substances – particularly opioids. At the time of our research, a hearing still hadn't been set to determine if the injunction would be permanent.

In press releases from U.S. Attorney Donald Cochran, prosecutors said that Oakley Pharmacy Inc., known as Dale Hollow Pharmacy, and Xpress Pharmacy of Clay County LLC, "illegally filled thousands of opioid and other prescriptions without a legitimate medical purpose." This resulted in two dead and many more hospitalized for overdoses.

In court documents and a Justice Department press release dated February 8th, 2019, Cochran said that Thomas Weir, who owns both pharmacies, oversaw operations and pharmacists Michael Griffith, John Polston, and Larry Larkin, all of whom are alleged to have illegally filled prescriptions for opiates. If true, it represents a complete failure to play the role pharmacists are supposed to. According to Cochran, that is to act as the "last line of defense before a controlled substance that was prescribed without any legitimate medical purpose is sold to a patient."

"The action supported today by the Drug Enforcement Administration should serve as a warning to those in the pharmacy industry who choose to put profit over customer safety," says D. Christopher Evans, special agent in charge of DEA's Louisville Field Division.

Sadly, such efforts may not have the widespread impact needed to change the trajectory of the opiate crisis. In the Tri-State area, the pattern remains the same despite increased restrictions and law enforcement attention. Addicts from other towns and states drive into these small towns to stock up, both for use and for resale. When new laws mandated tamper-proof pills and prescription regulations, illegal drug dealers stepped up and offered a cheaper and more accessible opioid: heroin. On the street, heroin is rarely sold in its pure form, typically being "cut down" with other substances in order to increase a dealer's inventory. Beyond a certain point, the injection fails to offer its user sufficient satisfaction, so today cheap heroin is often supplemented with extremely dangerous and powerful synthetic opioids such as fentanyl. These can be cheaper to manufacture and offer a powerful high, but are exceptionally dangerous because users cannot easily establish the concentration prior to injecting themselves with a potentially lethal overdose.

* * *

In February of 2018, three US Attorneys for the Tri-State area and representatives of the DEA, ATF, FBI, and state and local law enforcement agencies all gathered together in Ashland, Kentucky, just a few miles from the three way border. Attendees included Robert M. Duncan, Jr., of the Eastern District of Kentucky; Michael B. Stuart, of the Southern District of West Virginia; and Benjamin C. Glassman, of the Southern District of Ohio.

The working group focused its efforts on individuals responsible for violent crimes and significant drug trafficking activities in the area. As part of the collaborative partnership, members of ATF, FBI, DEA, and state and local law enforcement personnel agreed to share intelligence, and to review cases about the most dangerous drug trafficking offenders in the area.

"The good people of the Tri-State and good cities like Huntington, Ashland, Ironton and Portsmouth, have paid too high a price because of violent crime and the drug scourge. Effective partnerships, sharing resources and intelligence, and aggressive enforcement are the best offense to defeat those that bring chaos and despair to our communities," Stuart said at the time in an interview. "Now is the time to take our streets back from violent offenders and drug dealers that cause havoc. We are committed to working together as true partners in this fight to reduce violent crime, protect our citizens, and put dangerous criminals behind bars for as long as possible."

Thus began a year-long and earnest effort to tackle narcotics trafficking in the region. The governor of West Virginia, Jim Justice, even called in the West Virginia National Guard to support the counter-narcotics program in Huntington.

Guardsmen flew UH-72 Lakota helicopters on recon missions working with local police and providing eyes in the sky during busts and while serving warrants. Soldiers and technical military specialists provided both tech and analytical support, doing everything from working telephone hotlines and creating computer networks inside the Huntington Police Department's Criminal Investigation Bureau. They would help track down dealers and drug networks so cops can focus on the street.

It took sustained effort, but there were gains, at least on the surface. Only time will tell if the project can positively affect the situation, but the numbers remain grim even when they show improvement.

Initially there was a solid impact. Between 2017 and 2018, the city saw a 20 percent drop in violent crime and a 12 percent drop in property crime, according to Huntington Police.

"A key element we changed is that we now target specific individuals who are known to be violent drug offenders for rapid investigation. We arrest them for the other crimes they are committing before they become the trigger person," Dial told the *Huntington Herald-Dispatch* at the time. "We no longer allow them to linger in our community while selling drugs."

Dial further said that a lot of it wouldn't have been possible without the police department's relationship with the multijurisdictional task force, which wasn't sustainable in the long run.

One of the biggest actions that came out of the partnering was Operation Saigon Sunset. In that action in April 2018, about 200 officers and agents executed lightning raids across West Virginia, Ohio and Michigan, smashing an interconnected drug ring that had been operating in the tri-state area for fifteen years. Nearly one hundred suspects were awakened to teams battering in doors while National guard helicopters circled overhead.

That same month, federal agents and local and state police also executed another raid on what was called the "Peterson Drug Trade Operation," a Detroit-to-Huntington drug trafficking pipeline and in which agents seized what they said at the time was "fentanyl to kill a quarter million people."

It was all great news and better headlines, but locals we spoke about a year after the raids said that they hadn't made any real dent in the supply of illegal drugs to the area. Others wondered quietly how it was a major drug ring like the Peterson gang was able to operate for fifteen years in Huntington, and it only took two months for law enforcement to round them up.

"The D Boys haven't slowed down a bit. Maybe they're being a little quieter, but they're setting up shop long-term in Huntington, and maybe they're being smart about not making as much noise as before," says one man we interviewed. He's currently in recovery and spoke to us at the Waffle House in Catlettsburg, Kentucky, which lies in Boyd County, just across the state line from West Virginia.

* * *

It's a week night in Huntington, and we're with the HPD drug unit. They're making a series of warrant raids. Narcotics officers and uniformed officers are decked out in tactical gear. Every door-knock and every breach bring another adrenaline rush, but there's a weariness to the face of these officers. They've all been here before, too many times, and we can't but wonder about their morale. The task of arresting their way out of this crime wave seems Sisyphean and the faces of these officers confirm they know it from long exposure.

The apartments and homes they raid bring similar scenes of big screen TVs and game consoles set amidst dingy couches. Overflowing ashtrays on dirty coffee tables. Old takeout containers and skinny guys with bad tattoos, sleeveless T-shirts, and brand new sneakers. Women with dead eyes. Sour smells and squalor.

It all runs together after a while. Fewer dealers on the street is a good thing, but these aren't the big traffickers. These aren't the major players from Detroit gangs like the Seven Mile Bloods, Cash Out Crips, or the Hustle Boys. These are just foot soldiers. Nor are they the ones who traffic in the narcotics from outside the United States to supply these gangs.

A dozen people were arrested barely a month ago in a house off Madison Avenue here where police found heroin, crack cocaine and marijuana. Less than a month later, local dealers are back to business as usual, setting up shop just a few blocks down the street.

One officer mutters a phrase you hear way too often in the world of opioids. You hear it from people in law enforcement, criminal justice, and in treatment and rehabilitation. He looks weary when he says, "One step forward, two steps back."

"The profit motive is just too strong," one of the officers says during a break in the action. "The traffickers from Detroit make a connection in these areas, get a feel for the current drug trade and what the prices are and send in people to set up shop," he says. "The low-level members either get caught up like this or they get established and set up a bigger network. Then the higher-ups come in and build on that."

"A pill they get up in Cincinnati or Detroit that they get for ten dollars there can be sold for five times that here," he says. "They can markup heroin just the same. So they keep coming."

* * *

We're taken back to one of the words Hardin kept using when we talked, "Rot." It's not just that opioid abuse rots the minds and bodies of the users. It rots everything around the trade. Police come in and make arrests, but it's like using furniture polish on wood that's rotting from the inside out. This stuff corrupts everything it touches.

Ashland has just 26,000 residents, and it's a mostly White and working-class town. The downtown has a quaint little park with dozens of little restaurants and shops along the main avenue, which runs parallel to the Ohio River. Last year, in a moment of irony, students from Ashland Middle School won the national Samsung "Solve for Tomorrow" contest. Their winning design was a container that could be used to safely pick up used syringes, like the kind they would find on their playground. Police departments from several cities have contracted with the school for the design of the boxes, which can be manufactured on a 3D printer.

"In our area, we have a very big opioid crisis and there's a problem with people leaving around syringes," Aubree Hay, a seventh grader at Ashland Middle School, told media when the school won.

It's hard to gauge how pervasive the problem is, but both police and social workers say it's a consistent path for addicted women. First, they sleep with dealers for their fix. Then they turn to the streets, even in smaller towns like Huntington. The West Virginia Human Trafficking Task Force is trying to figure out the size and scope of the problem, but right now there's no hard data. However, prostitution cases intersect strongly with drug charges, and the children of these women are straining the state's foster care system.

Just up the road from Ashland is Portsmouth, Ohio, a small town of 20,000 founded in the late 1700s on the site of a former Shawnee village. It has been for the last twenty years a regular stop for presidential campaigns, a symbol of small-town Rust Belt America struggling to survive in the modern era. Back in the 1940s when the population was twice what it is today, Portsmouth was known as America's shoemaking capital.

It's also home to attorney Michael Mearan, a seventy-three-year-old former city councilman who was the target of a federal wiretap affidavit initially uncovered by the *Cincinnati Enquirer* in mid-March. The eighty-page affidavit filed in 2015 claimed that Mearan, described by the *Cincinnati Enquirer* as "a jowly, silver-haired attorney" who at the time was still practicing law, was also a "prolific sex trafficker." Over several decades, the affidavit alleges, Mearan supplied young, female clients with drugs "in exchange for and as an incentive to participate in acts of prostitution."

While Mearan was never charged, the newspaper reported that he remains under investigation by several agencies, and the fact that he's been known to law enforcement since the 1970s fuels suspicion by locals of collusion in the offices of power and the courts, or at the least a lack of concern between those in the halls of power and those who inhabit the forgotten Rust Belt byways and towns of Middle America. The rot is as much a metaphor for trust as it is a physical description of what opioids do to human flesh.

• • •

In Ashland, the Boyd County Detention Center has been a blight for years. People are pinning their hopes on the new jailer after the abrupt resignation of Joe Burchett in December 2018.

Burchett, sixty-eight, was indicted in February 2018 by a grand jury for "willfully neglecting the discharge of his official duties" as a public officer, but he wasn't removed as jailer until December 2018 when he lost election.

Under his watch in just his last months there were three different drug overdoses. The year before, also under his watch, eight women overdosed on heroin while in custody. William Alexander Mauk, a deputy jailer was arrested for supplying drugs and syringes to prisoners.

"People can get drugs in jail, but not like this," Rhonda Hardin tells us. We're at a family restaurant downtown talking over heaping plates of country vegetables and Irish stew. "This isn't some big state or federal prison, this is just the county jail. This wasn't within the bounds of normal.

"This is all about money to these people. They don't have souls," Hardin says. Her voice almost cracks from the frustration and her small hands are in tight fists. "It's all about their blood money. They don't care that they're destroying our people."

After she lost her bid for a city commissioner seat, she's continued her Cassandra-like quest to get people in the community to pay more attention to a drug crisis that has taken so many members of her family, and so many more of their friends.

But it's weighing on her soul. The single mother of two teenage daughters is considering moving down to Texas or Florida as soon as they're both in college. She has family down there. These hills and hollows are her home though, even if they've rotted from the inside, destroyed by an addictive poison that never should have been legal.

"I don't know," she says wearily, "I just don't know what to do."

5
Fighting Back

Part of the challenge of covering the opioid plague, from a writer's perspective, is the crazily fast pace of the events unfolding all around us. This week brought a quarter-million dollar meth and heroin bust in the small town of Ashland, Kentucky, where we were just a month ago. The bust only happened because a woman called the police to complain about a dog attacking her cat. When police arrived, the drug evidence was in plain sight. Then there was the west Kentucky constable arrested for stealing EMS drugs. A mother in Lexington snorted heroin and crashed her car with her four children in the back seat. We now get daily overdose reports from each of the counties we've visited. And now, there's the growing outbreak of Hepatitis C and HIV in these rural, working class communities.

It's impossible to cover every single event, drug bust, or health crisis driven by the use of opiates. There are simply too many. We're trying to focus on one little piece of the world at a time and tell stories one person at a time.

So, we've been encamped in Lexington, Kentucky and Cincinnati, Ohio, for several weeks. We've talked to police, community outreach leaders, business owners, and health care workers. We've spoken to those most victimized by this crisis: the addicts, the dependents, and those driven to sell body and soul to feed their habit. Our focus at the moment is on how law enforcement is struggling to deal with this monster and how it's changing how police approach their job.

The opioid crisis that engulfed these two small cities first came in the form of the pills, going back to the early 2000s. After the crackdown on the pill mills and the Florida pipeline in the first part of this decade, heroin made it onto the scene, followed quickly by synthetic opioids like fentanyl. Where the pills drained the soul of the people in places like Lexington and Cincinnati, the second wave of heroin and synthetics caused the overdose and death rate to skyrocket.

Fentanyl is the newest killer on the block here. Mixed with both heroin and cocaine, it alone constituted 763 overdose deaths in 2017, according to state records.

How bad is this on the street level? Fayette County, home of Lexington, celebrated a milestone in mid-May. For the first time in four years, Fayette County first responders went an entire day without having to use Narcan to revive any citizens. One day in four years. It only lasted a day.

But it's not just the overdose deaths; it's the rates of addiction and the toll that it all takes on individuals and communities in terms of broken lives, broken families, lost jobs, and existential despair. There is also tremendous collateral damage. Kentucky health officials say that opioid and meth abuse are contributing to a 30 percent rise in STDs in the state. That's because opioid users are at greater risk of contracting communicable diseases. These addicts are more likely to engage in unsafe behavior, like sharing needles and having unprotected sex. What's more, new hepatitis C cases from intravenous drug use are now roughly triple the number of new HIV cases from the same source. Kentucky and West Virginia are leading America when it comes to new hepatitis C cases, and if left untreated, hepatitis C can be fatal.

Kentucky also has the nation's second-highest rate of parents who are incarcerated. And as a consequence, Kentucky has the nation's highest rate of grandparents or other relatives raising children. Fully 9 percent of kids in the Bluegrass State are being raised by a relative.

Nationally, it's just 4 percent.

* * *

Newtown Police Chief Thomas Synan has seen this time and again. Newtown is a little suburban village on the east side of Cincinnati with less than three thousand citizens. It's an extremely homogenous community of almost 97 percent non-Hispanic Whites with a median age of thirty-nine and a median household income of $59,800.

It's the home of the Hamilton County Heroin Coalition. The coalition is made up of law enforcement, health care and community leaders in and around the Cincinnati metropolitan area trying to get a handle on the opioid crisis with a more holistic approach to enforcement, treatment, and rehabilitation.

Synan is a compact, muscular man, every bit the tough-as-iron Marine he was back in his youth. He's over fifty now but doesn't show it except for the salt and pepper in his hair. On his right arm he has a tattoo of the Marine Corps motto, "Semper Fi," meaning "Ever Faithful." On his left arm is the word "Sheepdog," a reference to an essay by Lt. Col. Dave Grossman after 9/11:

> *If you have no capacity for violence then you are a healthy productive citizen: a sheep. If you have a capacity for violence and no empathy for your fellow citizens, then you have defined an aggressive sociopath—a wolf. But what if you have a capacity for violence, and a deep love for your fellow citizens? Then you are a sheepdog, a warrior, someone who is walking the hero's path.*

Synan's small office is decorated with framed newspaper clippings and his own opinion essays. There's also a lot of Batman and GI Joe paraphernalia, as well as a gallon of water and some protein powder. Synan's been quoted everywhere from the *BBC* to *Rolling Stone* and

Time magazine. He has spoken to the White House on a number of occasions trying to bring more attention to the opioid epidemic.

"Law enforcement is at a crossroads," Synan tells us. "Are we law enforcement or first responders? I think we have to be both, even if we don't want to be. We feel like we're constantly in emergency mode and we're wondering why this isn't more of a priority—the priority."

For Synan, who joined this little village's police department in 1993 and worked both drugs and SWAT before rising in the ranks, it all began with one family in Newtown—the Millers.

Off and on, Synan and the Newtown Police Department have been dealing with the Millers since he joined the force. The mother and her three sons had thick files in the Newtown Police records, chalking up complaints and arrests for trespassing, domestic disputes, suicide threats, domestic violence, public intoxication, petty thefts, burglaries, robberies, and, of course, drugs and drug paraphernalia.

The mother, Sharon Berwinger Miller, operated as a single parent. The father of her three sons lived homeless in Hamilton County. After years of struggling with addiction, she died on July 4th, 2006 from alcohol and opioid pills. Her death came just months after her youngest, Josh Miller, aged twenty-five, died during a shoot-out in a crack cocaine buy in Cincinnati. Her oldest son Jonathan died eight years later of an overdose on September 23rd, 2014, aged just thirty-nine. Jonathan had five children and a wife who was also an addict. On November 25th, 2014, Synan's officers responded to a call of an overdose. It was Charles Miller, who they revived with naloxone. But he died the next morning from an overdose, having left care and returned home to shoot up. He was thirty-five.

Now, Synan says, some of the children of the three brothers are caught up in opioid addiction and the cascading effect of crime. "Three generations in one family lost to this," he says. "In this small little village. It told me what we're doing isn't working. You can't punish the addiction out of someone and you can't arrest your way out of this crisis."

"I mean, I would like to focus on the arrests. Arresting the dealers, but spending our time going after the addicts and putting them in the criminal justice system isn't getting us anywhere. Addiction is a mental health problem. And we're police. We want to be arresting the bad guys, not people with mental health problems."

After the death of Charles Miller, Synan took the unprecedented step of writing an essay about the tragic tale of the Miller family which was published in the *Cincinnati Enquirer* in December 2014 titled "Why Care About Another Dead Addict?"

Synan soon found himself thrust into the spotlight in the national conversation that law enforcement leaders were having with themselves about their proper role and approach in dealing with the opioid crisis. He was invited to national and international law enforcement conferences, joining the debate among frustrated police department brass who were, and still are, overwhelmed by the scope of the opioid menace.

"Right now, law enforcement is working both criminal enforcement and the mental health problem just by default. And we want someone to take that second part out of our hands," he said. "We should be focusing on the supply side: the dealers. While the medical community needs to be taking over getting the users help. But they're not doing that so we're stuck with both duties."

We stop Synan for second. "How do you define 'dealer'?" we ask.

Most cops we've talked to by now have zero interest in simple users, except perhaps as potential informants. They have almost as little interest in the addict who has the foresight and extra cash to buy his own stash plus a little more to sell to friends. Who is the guy that cops really want to get off the street and into the jail?

The way his eyes light up it's almost like he's saying "gotcha."

"That's just it. What is a drug dealer? The pharmaceutical companies, just like the guy out on the street corner—they both give out free samples. They both brand their product. They both market," Synan says. "You tell me the difference.

"Law enforcement saw this opioid crisis coming. We saw it with the prescription pills ten to fifteen years ago. You asked why it so predominantly hit Caucasians instead of African-Americans. This may have been the one time in history it was unhealthier to have health insurance than not have it," he says. "Ten to fifteen years ago we started having people coming in reporting that someone stole their OxyContin. And they'd be in the next week. And the next week. We started realizing they were just getting the police reports to turn into their doctor to get another prescription filled."

Then came the heroin. Then came the fentanyl. It was actually one of the Miller grandchildren in 2016 that told Newtown cops about "China white," a street name for fentanyl, hitting their village. They hadn't even heard of it until then. Not long after, in eight days Hamilton County saw twenty-five overdoses, with one or two overdose deaths per day.

"Here we are trying to do street buys of narcotics and you have legal entities pushing legal pills, or you have China just shipping in fentanyl. Trade wars don't kill anyone but the fentanyl trade from China is killing tens of thousands. I can't go to China. I have three square miles where I have authority," he says. "We need to have programs for the health care and medical industry to take care of people with addiction problems, while police focus on the supply side. Addiction comes from a combination of trauma, genetics, and environment. How is a cop supposed to do anything with that?

"And let me say this, I think if we partnered better with state and federal authorities we could do something about the supply. That's what we should be doing. I don't believe it's demand—people addicted to drugs—that solely creates the supply. I'm on my tenth version of iPhone and I didn't ask for nine. We can make a difference if we go at this properly," Synan says.

He's written to President Donald Trump, asking him to put the opioid crisis front and center and end it. Synan believes a president has the power to make it a national cause, like the race to get to the moon or the effort to wipe out polio or AIDS.

"So, it costs us $100 billion or more over the next ten years—what has this cost us already? How many lives? Plus $30-$50 billion in productivity? It's the leading cause of death for people under fifty," he asks. "You know how much medical training I have? How much doctor training? Zero. We all have to get involved to solve this and it will cost us. But not solving this will cost us more. The president could lead the way in helping us change how we deal with drug addiction and drug crime. He once declared this a national health emergency. But all there has been is words, no action."

* * *

Lexington, Kentucky is just a little over an hour south of Synan's stomping grounds. It's a place of remarkable history and beauty. It was settled in 1775 in the Inner Bluegrass region, and today it has a city population of over 323,000 plus a metropolitan area population of more than half a million. It ranks at the same spot on two distinctive lists—as tenth in cities with the highest college education rate; and is listed by Forbes as the tenth cleanest city in the United States. The median income is almost $50,000.

The economy here is diverse enough that it wasn't hit as hard as eastern Kentucky by the coal mine closings over the past two decades, or as hard as other comparable size cities by the housing crash of 2007–2008. We find a little nugget of information about the city that catches our eye: in 1935, the Addiction Research Center was created as a small research unit at the U.S. Public Health Service Hospital in Lexington. It was founded as one of the first drug rehabilitation clinics in the nation.

The city itself is surrounded by gorgeous horse farms—don't call them ranches. They're bordered by white hardwood fences that look like something out of a painting. Breeders here raise thoroughbreds and dream of racing at Churchill Downs, or having a horse sire a champion racer. It's a big enough place to have a variety of restaurants, shopping, and entertainment venues. But it still feels small enough that going across town doesn't take all day and neighbors seem to know one another. Money from a combination of the business community, University of Kentucky alumni organizations, and the multigenerational families of horse patricians help the city boast a professional orchestra, two ballet companies, several museums and choirs, and an acclaimed opera program at the University of Kentucky.

We are, unfortunately, not near any of that. Or seeing anything so uplifting. We're parked in front of a convenience store at the corner of Seventh Street and Maple on the east side of Lexington. We've been here about two hours and it's been a never-ending parade of everything from the most desperate prostitutes to people clearly doing a heroin shamble up and down the street. There's a look both addicts and prostitutes give passing cars, a yearning stare searching for any opportunity—a hand out, an offer, something. We pull up at four thirty on a Thursday afternoon and the despair here is on full display. It's a stark contrast to the bucolic horse farms just a few miles away.

For the last fifteen minutes we've been watching a shirtless man straddling a teal mountain bike. He's hanging around the front of a ramshackle convenience store. The signage advertises cheap tacos, the likes of which we won't be trying. Just yesterday, on the wealthy southwest side of town, a young man living with his parents in a seven-figure McMansion overdosed and was saved. But that's all kept behind closed doors when it's addiction at that level. That's where many pills still circulate and the heroin is more likely to be of a higher quality.

At the lower end, where we are, it's literally all out in the street. The man on the bike alternates between looking around and nodding off while standing up. Every once in a while, a car passing through the narrow intersection will honk and startle him awake. Three times Lexington Police marked cars come through the intersection, but they take little notice of him. This poor soul isn't a priority.

A well-dressed, younger black man in his early twenties in a printed shirt and dark jeans pulls a van up across the intersection from where I'm staked out. The sky is threatening to rain but it holds off. He breaks out a folding table and sets up a stand. We can't see what the van says but we're curious. As we approach the van, the shirtless biker rides down the sidewalk and crashes into a chain link fence, falling over. He gets up and peddles down the street again.

The young black man finishes setting up the table and we exchange a headshake and introductions. His name is Aaron Ashby-Boyd, and he works as an HIV prevention specialist for a non-profit called "AVOL"—AIDS Volunteers Inc. He and others regularly go to these hotspots and set up to provide mobile HIV screenings, free condoms, and information for people caught up on the street. That's how bad it is in this part of town. He'll end up setting up at another two drug and prostitution hotspots before the night is out.

Ashby-Boyd is not a volunteer. This is his full-time job. And, of course, he has his own history with addiction. "I've been clean six years now. I went through a program and now I have my life in order. I have a job, a wife and kids, but it wasn't easy," he says, stuffing some brochures into a tabletop holder.

We ask him what his "drug of choice" was, a phrase we've learned is common parlance for those in recovery. "Pills. I was driving vans down to Florida on my learner's permit in high school," he says. And there it is. We can't seem to turn a corner in this part of the world without meeting someone caught up in this. And so few of the stories have an ending as happy as Ashby-Boyd's.

We know this because of what unfolds over the days we spend with the Lexington Police narcotics unit, the Crisis Intervention Team, and Lexington's unique, but small, paramedicine unit. We know this because of the time I'll spend with a restaurant owner and his wife, who are trying to make a dent in the opioid crisis with a business opportunity. We know it because of some of the things we have already seen and heard in recent weeks. Stories we will never unhear and events we will never unsee.

* * *

We're having lunch with Lt. Patrick Branam at a place called DV8 Kitchen in southwest Lexington. He's got a handlebar moustache, wears Gargoyle sunglasses and greets everyone with a hug. The son of a Baptist minister, he's married with two boys and we suspect the most common phrase he ever speaks is "I love you, brother." He's been a firefighter and EMT since 2005, and has served as a sheriff's deputy.

He's also part of a pilot system that Lexington started using, a $650,000, post-9/11 federal grant program that pushes community healthcare beyond its current limits. It's a lot like what Chief Synan seemed to be talking about, or near enough to it. The program isn't designed solely for dealing with drug addiction, but you can bet that's a major focus of its efforts.

Here's how it works. Paramedics visit the homes of patients who tend to most often use the ambulance service to be taken to the emergency room. The Lexington Fire Department's eleven ambulances responded to 48,238 medical calls in 2017, with just 266 people accounting for 8.9 percent of those calls. Medical run volume for the department grew an average of 7.5 percent each year for the last three years.

"We were dealing with what we call 'friendly faces and familiar places,'" he says around a bite of his burger. "So instead of just dealing with the immediate medical issue, we follow up with them and visit them at home, or in shelters, or even on the street—trying to get to the root problem," Branam says. "Whether it's education, getting them resources for drug rehabilitation or housing, or just getting them to a treatment facility that accepts their insurance, we are both helping them and freeing up health care resources."

He's not exaggerating. A year after the program started in February

2018, Lexington ambulance runs were down 2 percent. The previous three years saw an increase of more than 22 percent. The program now has more than one hundred community partners, with both the police and local courts on board because of the impact they've seen it makes.

"The thing that is missing in community and emergency health care—and especially with drug dependence—is taking that next step after the acute condition is resolved," he says. "We have to start thinking in terms of how do we do the next right thing for the person in front of us. You can't take care of somebody if you don't know their story. As a firefighter I have to know what a wall is made of if I want to break through it, and it's the same with helping people."

Firefighters and paramedics, like cops, tend toward the callous side in that they have to be thick-skinned given what they see and deal with every day. At first some of his colleagues razzed him. "They'd say 'Here comes the hug brigade,' but I would laugh and go, 'Yeah, but when's the last time you had to treat X patient, and how many runs did you go on last month compared to last year?' They're realizing this works," Branam says. "You have to find that gap, that human need not being met and it can change things."

The program also takes traditional calls and develop relationships with people on the street or on the fringes. On one call he treats a woman who has been working the streets. She twisted her ankle running from a customer who was beating her. She looks at him and says, "You're the first man who touched me who didn't want something from me." She takes his card and some information he has for a ministry called Natalie's Sisters, which provides assistance for women working prostitution or in strip clubs. Maybe she'll make it there.

Later we drive by the county detention center together. "This is where so many of the people I see could have their direction changed—when they walk out of here. Most of them walk right back into their habits, their bad relationships and their addictions. If we could stop them here and give them a new way, we might see a lot less repeat traffic coming in and out of here," Branam says.

On a visit to a wooded area just off Scott Street and Oliver Lewis across from a repo business, there are a dozen or so people camped out on the grounds. He's got bottled water and information for anyone who wants to follow up with him and get help—be it medical, housing, job, rehab, or anything else.

"The neighbors don't even know anyone is camped out here until winter, when the foliage dies and people can see them. Then we get complaints," Branam says.

If it seems like Branam is a serial do-gooder, it's a fair assessment. But the numbers back him up and the program is saving money, if not lives. Still, we ask Branam what it was that brought him this almost annoyingly upbeat attitude. No one should be this perpetually optimistic given what he sees on a daily basis.

In the relatively few weeks we've spent with the Lexington police, EMTs, and firefighters, we saw a close friend of a source overdose and die, we saw a mother who overdosed in front of her twin thirteen-month-old babies, and we witnessed the rescue of a girl being sex trafficked while kept high as her pimp rented her out to dozens of men.

But what Branam describes next leaves us chilled. If they've worked the job long enough, paramedics, firefighters, and police often have a single moment on the job that defines things for them. It often haunts them forever. It affects them in ways most civilians can never understand. He pulls the car to a stop and looks us in the eye.

"I got called one day. Not too long ago, to help an ambulance crew. The lady in this house had been dead for two days. An overdose. She had a kid maybe two years old. She was in a full diaper and she was playing with three McDonalds Happy Meal toys. Her mother's body was in the den on the couch. They got the kid out of there and I was looking at the body. She was slumped back and there was milk that had run down her lips," Branam says, his voice choking and tears in his eyes. "She was trying to feed her mom some milk to get her up."

It takes a moment for Branam to get his composure back. "Things have to change," he says. "We measure success an hour at a time."

* * *

This is the unsexy part of the fight against the opioid crisis. It's a sunny mid-May afternoon and three cops, a business developer from Landmark Recovery, and six women in various fields of healthcare are having the monthly advisory board meeting for the Crisis Intervention Training program. It's an ongoing program that tries to bridge the gap between what police know and deal with and what healthcare professionals know and deal with. Most all new recruits and most of the veterans of the Lexington Police Department have gone through an initial crisis intervention training.

It sounds basic, but the two fields have their own languages and jargons, and they have crossover acronyms that decidedly don't mean the same thing. There's a lot of "not it" played when it comes to the no-man's land that is a hospital or mental health center waiting room. Cops can get stuck all day dealing with people who should be patients, and health care workers can be stuck dealing with patients who should be in handcuffs.

This is not hypothetical. They talk at length about a recent case where a police officer brought in a patient to a mental health facility that should have been admitted but who then took a swing at an officer. It ended up tying up both center personnel and the police past five o'clock the following morning.

The board also shares intelligence and knowledge, fully within patient privacy, on what they're seeing in the hospital versus what police are seeing on the street. "We're seeing a rise in LSD, almost always among the THC users," one of the women in scrubs says.

Sgt. Brian Martin, who heads up the Lexington Police narcotics unit, takes a note. That's useful to know. He and the head of the

University of Kentucky PD are here along with another Lexington Police detective, Alejandro "Zack" Zaglul, bureau of special operations, who works as a liaison to the fire department's Community Paramedicine program.

Martin doesn't look like a narcotics cop, or what you think a narcotics cop should look like based on movies and television. He looks more like a suburban softball coach who makes dad jokes and plays too much Fleetwood Mac. He's balding but close cropped with a blond goatee. He's in his early forties and he's a voracious history reader. His blue eyes are bright and he smiles easily, but there's a soulful sadness in them as well. He wears dad jeans, short sleeve shirts, and comfortable hiking boots. If you have an eye for it, you can usually tell when someone, police or civilian, is wearing a concealed weapon. You can't tell with Martin.

Martin has been with the Lexington Police for about fourteen years. When we first met him, it was at a destination restaurant in downtown Lexington called Saul Good. He'd been meeting with the owner Rob Perez. The two collaborate on a number of community outreach programs outside of but related to Martin's work.

Perez is a well-known Lexington restaurateur who owns Saul Good. It's an upscale, New American restaurant. He's also a devout Christian and a recovering alcoholic who has been sober for twenty-eight years. We lose count of the number of community boards, church missions, and non-profits that he and his wife, Diane, are part of. But an important one is Natalie's Sisters, a Christian outreach for women caught up in prostitution or other sex work and the addiction that typically accompanies it.

Martin and Perez met because of Natalie's Sisters. The organization was conceived following the tragic murder of a young prostitute in Lexington, who was prototypically caught up in the cycle of addiction and sex work. On January 1st, 2012, Natalie, a strip club dancer and prostitute known to both police and to community outreach workers, was murdered by her "boyfriend" and pimp.

Martin was a lower rank at the time but he knew of her. Perez's wife was part of the "Bruised Reed" ministry, a Christian group that Natalie had occasionally talked to.

Martin and Perez worked with others and wrote up the business plan for a non-profit outreach named "Natalie's Sisters" in her honor. The help it offers and the little steps it takes are designed to lead girls away from that life of exploitation and addiction.

Perez and Martin are just two of the drivers in the interconnected world of community leaders, police, first responders, business owners, and advocates in Lexington. This network is strong, but by their own admission they're just barely making a dent. Every little bit counts, though. Over the course of several hours at Saul Good, Perez and Martin talk about all the initiatives they're involved in.

About a year after Natalie's death, in 2013, Perez and his wife found a burnt spoon in the trash at Saul Good. "Our best server was doing heroin in the bathroom, during her shift. Cooking and shooting up," Perez says.

They started counting up the butcher's bill of addiction in just their one little restaurant. They'd lost more than a dozen employees to addiction, half to opioids, in just ten years. The first manager they'd hired had died in jail after getting busted trying to get opioid pills. They'd had a cook die of an overdose. The list went on and on.

"My wife is what really drove this. Some men in my Bible group didn't even believe we could be having this kind of problem in Lexington, but we decided we had to do what we could for our own people," Perez says. "I mean, I was going to Indonesia for mission work, but what was I doing in my own hometown for my people?"

With $300,000 in capital raised from community members and partners, Perez founded DV8 Kitchen, a unique breakfast and lunch grill just southwest of downtown. Of the twenty-eight employees, all but one is in active recovery. The rules are strict because restaurant work is so tied to the alcohol and drug lifestyle. The hours run late and shifts are flexible. There are cash tips and the work usually doesn't require background checks or drug tests. Employees often have access to the bar.

DV8 employees have to be in active recovery programs and submit to regular testing. There's no tolerance for being late or missing shifts. Tips are pooled and are paid through direct deposit, reducing the temptation that cash has for an addict. There's ongoing life coaching and counseling that's mandatory for all employees.

DV8 is a hip, garage-like space in a strip mall within walking distance of the area's three largest rehabilitation centers. Local artists painted the walls with graffiti. You can watch employees lovingly kneading and shaping the dough for the bakery through the open kitchen. It's all burgers and salads and bakery items. At DV8, there's no bar.

It works. Despite the razor thin margins in the restaurant industry, DV8 is profitable. Perez says he'd run it at a loss, but it's good to make a profit too. And the turnover is barely one-fifth of the industry standard. It's a small step, but it's a step forward.

"Think about what we've been doing about addiction for the last fifty years? Arrest them. Put them in jail. Give them a record. Turn them out to the streets with almost no chance of getting a job, very little in the way of rehab or recovery programs. What the fuck do you think that's going to accomplish?" Perez says.

Martin nods in agreement. "There's got to be a different way. In narcotics we want to go after traffickers. And that's what we do. But we have to work with people like Rob to start tearing down what drives that demand. When we come across someone on a call who is on drugs, we have to start asking 'How did we get here?'" Martin continues, "That's a hard question for a cop, but one we have to start asking."

Perez tells us about how he and Martin have gone to the Lexington City Council to try to get more funds for programs to engage the opioid crisis at the street level. Martin engages the drug war going after traffickers, after all, but he also believes this war has to be fought on multiple fronts.

"We get told that they might have the funding next year," Perez says. "We're at the center of this thing in this part of the country." He looks disgusted. "We see overdose deaths and the collateral damage of addiction every day, and we're still waiting for maybe getting funding."

Over the next few hours Perez and Martin talk about all the strategies they would like to see in place to help curb addiction on the demand side—job and life skill training, ways to cut out the red tape and penny-ante conviction enforcement that keeps marginalized people caught up in the justice system. They talk through a dozen other ways to break the cycle.

Perez has to leave early, but Martin continues talking. He's driven in equal measures by a hatred of those who traffic opioid poisons and a compassion for those who are victims.

"I remember the case that really woke me up," he says. "There was a young girl. She was addicted. People like to blame addicts but they don't know what they're talking about. Yes, there's personal responsibility. Yes, many made that first choice to use, but can you hold that against them fifteen years later?"

"In this case, the girl was addicted because when she was twelve her mother held her down and shot her up with heroin, telling the girl she was doing it so she would know how to do it right," Martin says. He has a haunted look on his face. "She's nineteen now and working the streets."

Martin isn't some bleeding heart. He's a devout Christian, but to him working with people who are addicted and helping them are part of the totality of law enforcement. His narcotics unit doesn't go after users, but when users are arrested by patrol officers, they are the primary source of information that allows his officers to bust the traffickers.

In the meanwhile, his approach of encouraging officers to ask "How did we get here?" might get the user a step out of the cycle, or might help the officer build a better case.

"If your give-a-damn is broken, you're probably not going to be a good officer anyway," he says.

If he sounds soft on addicts, it's more than made up in his fury at the dealers. Kentucky recently increased mandatories for drug dealing, and when an overdose death can be directly linked to a specific dealer, it can bring a federal life sentence. "We need to put them all under the jail," he says through clenched teeth.

We talk for hours in that booth at Saul Good and then something remarkable happens. It's something that's been happening to us a lot lately. It's about four o'clock in the afternoon and the restaurant is largely dead anyway. A server who had been a booth away rolling up silverware in cloth napkins apologizes for interrupting and says she couldn't help but overhear what we're talking about.

"It just means so much for you to be so passionate about this," she says, tears welling in her eyes. She's around thirty, with a heartbeat tattoo on her forearm and short blonde hair. She's in recovery and her fiancé, who she met in rehab, just overdosed and died six weeks earlier. Her mother and father were both dead of overdoses and her brother is in "active addiction," meaning he's using. She's been to jail and her three children—two girls and one boy, all under thirteen— are with family. She's been clean and sober for twenty-one months. She wants to get custody back. She's been working every shift she can just to stay busy and focused, and because she's barely making ends meet now that she's alone.

"I just want to thank you for what you're doing," she tells Martin. Martin shares with her his own struggles with issues like depression, and asks her about what support she has and if she's going to meetings. He gives her his cell phone number and gets her name and date of birth. He's going to look into helping her dispose of a few parking tickets and then what can be done to help her get her children back, if she's willing. He's also going to hook her into his network of organizations and programs that might get her financial assistance.

She didn't ask for any help, she just expressed gratitude, but that's the kind of guy Martin is. There are a lot of tears around the table. Before she leaves to get back to work, Martin asks if he can pray with her. He takes her hand. The tears seem to be contagious.

After she leaves us, Martin makes a point that leaves us thunderstruck. "We lost what, 50,000 people last year to drug overdoses," he says. "If you changed the name of what killed them to something else—say, terrorism—do you think a year later we'd still be hoping to get funding to fight terrorism?"

6
Never-Ending Battle

We spend time with the Lexington Police narcotics unit over the next week and the things we see and hear will be with us a lifetime. The unit is located in a former strip mall on the east side of town, just inside the interstate loop. The detective bay for the eighteen officers plus their sergeants and lieutenant looks like any other corporate cubicle farm. That is, if you ignore the body armor hanging off the office chairs, the various flags on the walls, or the gun magazines in the bathroom.

Because of the nature of narcotics works and an agreement with the Lexington Police Department, we won't use the real names of any of the detectives, but we hang out with guys like "Eric" who is just a year in narcotics and expects he wants to retire from it rather than ever transferring or ranking up and out.

Eric started as a parole officer for the state and spent six years working for the Lexington PD. Until his transfer to narcotics, he was working first on patrol and then with the CLEAR unit. It's a proactive, elite uniformed unit that doesn't get bogged down in regular patrols and works as a farm team for the non-uniformed and SWAT divisions.

Eric is still building his network of "CIs." The Lexington department calls them "cooperating individuals," but other departments call them "confidential informants." CI networks are crucial for working narcotics. They're comprised mostly of users who get caught up in the criminal justice system and are willing to work with police to avoid harsh sentences. CIs will do controlled drug buys that are used to get warrants to arrest the traffickers and dealers. CIs are vetted—no violent or sexual abuse criminals are allowed. They have to sign agreements to not use or skim off the top.

Detectives spend hours developing CIs—befriending them without being their friends. They have to be managed, detectives say. They're natural con-men and will tell you want they think you want to hear if they think it will get them something. The idea of working CIs and then the dealers they bust, of course, is to work their way up the ladder. This means eventually cooperating with state and federal law enforcement, as well as other cities.

So far Eric's biggest bust in the past year was getting a dealer who had homicide charges in Detroit going back to 2012. These cops are meticulous about what they're doing because they want busts that will lead to convictions. And they have an incredibly high conviction rate.

One detective confides in us that even when there's a mistake or someone gets off, they consider it a win. "Let's say hypothetically an officer cut a corner and a dealer skates," he says. "It's not like the judge is going to say, 'Ok, I'm throwing out your arrest and the evidence against you. Here's your heroin back.' We're still getting 50 or a 100 grams off the street. How many lives will that save? One hundred grams is about a thousand dosage units."

These cops don't see as much in the way of pills as they used to. In the few weeks we're in Lexington, there are several overdoses from pills, but by and large those using pills here are in the middle and upper classes. Or they are those with legitimate chronic pain who can still afford to go to the doctors or who have access to the pain clinics.

Heroin and synthetics like fentanyl are now the primary street narcotics these cops see. Recently, they've seen a resurgence of crystal meth, which they ironically attribute to their successes in going after opioids. Street price for meth just three years ago was about $300 for an eight ball (an eighth of an ounce or 3-3.5 grams). Cartels, not local cooks, have been upping their imports, so now the price is down to $100 for an eight ball, Martin tells us.

Here's a thumbnail of how the drug traffic into Lexington works today. Detroit remains the primary source for heroin and fentanyl. A typical dealer is a "D Boy" who comes into town with about $6,000 worth of product on him. He'll inform his network of buyers that he's in town and where. He'll stay a week, make his sales, and head back north with about $10,000—clearing $4,000 for a week's work.

What we get to see though is that while these dealers are just a step above street thugs, they are savvy. We get to see that they're using things like Snapchat and Airbnb.

"We can develop sources at all the hotels. That's how they used to set up. Some still do. We can have people working at the hotels, especially along the interstate, who tip us off when they think there's something shady," Martin tells us. "But now they're starting to use Airbnb. They can set up in a property, never have to see anyone when they check in, and it's a hell of a lot harder for us to get the information on an Airbnb." While burner phones and group texts are still used, increasingly the dealers are using apps like Snapchat which make it harder for cops to intercept messages or collect evidence after.

There are also local dealers, who may be in the trade to make profits or simply to maintain their own habit. There's remarkably little in the way of competitive violence or "turf wars." Eric thinks that's largely because there's enough profit for everyone and they've learned that they don't want to draw the heat of public scrutiny with gang violence.

Consequently, cops are having to adapt. They've got it down to where they can have a CI make a controlled buy and within an hour have a signed warrant. Cases are often made in hours, not days or weeks. It's stressful because it leaves little room for error. They're executing between thirty-five and forty warrants a month.

What you see on those raids is soul-crushing. Children totally neglected in homes where there's dog feces all over the floor. A child playing with a toy car rolling it between the droppings. On one raid there's a stash of fentanyl hidden among the diapers next to a crib. Fentanyl is so powerful mere skin contact can cause an overdose. In another house, a local dealer has several twenty-gallon containers of Tide Pods. "Don't be surprised," Eric tells us. "Some of these guys work in barter. They'll put in whole shoplifting orders that their buyers will fill to get their fix."

There's one house where the cutting table, which is where the heroin is cut with anything from laxative to fentanyl, is within two feet of the baby's crib.

On one raid we observed, Lexington detectives sought both to arrest a dealer and to rescue a girl the dealer was trafficking. Martin found her ad through a system called Spotlight, a computer aggregation and sifting site that uses facial recognition to track online prostitution ads nationwide.

The LPD doesn't have an actual prostitution unit, but narcotics and prostitution go hand in hand, so Martin regularly trawls the data on Spotlight to look for potential trafficking victims. It's an art more than a science—he looks for certain aspects to posted pictures, or the map of where a girl has advertised. He or one of his detectives find a likely trafficking victim and end up texting to gather intel. "Some dealers find it more profitable to traffic girls than to sling dope," he says.

While we're there they bust a dealer who is also trafficking an underage girl. Shortly before we got to Lexington, Martin busted another dealer/pimp in a scene out of a horror movie. "They kept this girl hopped up constantly. In one weekend they ran about sixty guys through her," Martin says.

The most horrifying moment from our time in Lexington was not a bust, but an overdose death. While the narcotics unit is focused on building cases against dealers, they investigate every overdose and they have one detective entirely dedicated to backtracking every overdose to see if he can build a case. It's a long shot, but if he can make the case, it can bring a federal life sentence.

Both Martin and Eric tell us they have talked to dealers who admit they are aware of the law and that it has been a deterrent. But not in this case. It's an early May afternoon in a small home on the east side. Police were called for a welfare check. Narcotics was called because of what they discovered.

The inside has an unmistakable rank, repugnant, and rotting smell that's combined with a sickly sweet note. It's the smell of death. The resident has been dead two days. She died sitting at the kitchen table with a needle in her arm and slumped to the ground.

Mere feet away is a playpen. Her twin eighteen-month-old children were inside. As ghastly as it is, these children have been beside their dead mother for two days. It's a blessing that they were in the playpen, Martin tells us. He's choked up. Movies don't show cops crying, but they do.

"They would have crawled all over their mother trying to wake her. The needle was right beside her," he says. "I can only pray that they don't remember this."

Martin's soulful eyes grow angry. "I'm so sick of this," he says.

They focus on heroin and meth sales grow. They go after D Boys and local dealers step in. The ladder they try to climb in getting convictions bumps against a ceiling of jurisdictional limits. For every addict they help or dealer they bust, it's another day and another overdose.

"I do think I'm making a difference. I don't think we'll ever solve the drug problem but it's like everything else in this world. It's like world hunger or something. You have to keep trying because imagine how much worse it would be without us," Eric tells us. "You have to try. And we can take care of this end. We need people to take care of the other end and get these addicts help so there's no demand."

We're there on the day of Sergeant Jesse Palmer's last day in narcotics. He's being promoted to an administrative position, so it's okay to use his name. He's spent almost a decade working narcotics, starting with doing "trash pulls" with CLEAR. That's where officers obtain evidence from trash cans to generate probable cause and get a warrant. The former Marine is olive skinned, shaven headed, and has a perpetual light in his eyes and a smile on his face.

We ask him a question that's beginning to feel routine: "After all you've seen, how can you be so positive all the time?"

He smiles, "You can make a difference. It's a little at a time. But you take the legs out from under the street dealer in some neighborhood you, feel good when you walk through there. You're doing your service to the taxpayer," he says. "Will someone be there within a week or two dealing again? Yes." He shrugs, "But we make one dent here and another there. And if we weren't doing that—imagine how bad it would be."

* * *

During our time in Lexington, we met some of the most incredible people we've seen on the front line of this. We saw through their eyes the toll of the opioid crisis on their community, and everything they're doing to fight it.

We also saw something that has become almost normal since we started this project. The day after we met Rob Perez and Brian Martin at Saul Good and the day before we met Rob's wife, Diane, and Patrick Branam at DV8 Kitchen, one of Rob and Diane's former waiters died of an overdose.

"You don't have to look for hurt. Hurt will find you," Martin said.

We want to see this world up close and personal without a filter. Thanks to our time with the police, those working in outreach, and the community paramedicine team, we have a good handle on where the hotspots are.

So, we spend an evening along Seventh Street, dressed down in thrift shop clothes. We see a shirtless guy slumped over in his car and his friends trying to get him into the house. Hungry-eyed homeless—either by choice, mental illness, or as victims of the generally broken

American economic system—as well as prostitutes, ne'er-do-wells, and hustlers. Despite our best efforts, either we're sticking out like a sore thumb, or just imagining it, but it seems hard to get any conversation going with people here. We're pretty nervous and it probably shows.

The second evening it's almost eight o'clock and the sun is still up. We're in a park off Limestone Street by the Robert F. Stephens Courthouse. Across the way are some restaurants and bars with patios. Normal, happy people are dining and drinking. There's a fountain on one end of the park and some parents are watching kids cooling themselves off in the water fountain. We're in a part of the park that is decidedly less celebratory. There's a shirtless guy skateboarding. He's a skinny White guy in a headband and red Nike's. A couple of fat White girls are talking with some black men. There's a guy with a flowing white beard and baseball cap next to older dude in polo shirt and sunglasses. There's a look people who live on the street have. Hard to put into words, but they're not there enjoying the evening. They're working some angle or another.

This is where we meet "Red." That's the name he goes by. He used to be a University of Kentucky student. He dropped out just six years ago, he says, even though his face looks a lot more aged than thirty. He asks if we're "holding" and we tell him no. He doesn't ask for money or anything else so we take it he thinks we're also street addicts.

We ask him if he's holding and he says he's waiting for a friend to get in touch. We talk a while. Not sure how to play this and we don't want to spook him with too many questions. Eventually we get from him that he was a student and started using Adderall to study. He never smoked marijuana, but using Adderall got him hooked up with people who sold him Norco—an opiate. He got hooked on that and it spiraled from there. Now he's a heroin user. He's not homeless, but like a lot of users, he spends his time out on the street.

What he's telling us could all be true. Then again, it could be a self-serving lie, much like the stripper who tells customers she's working her way through medical school. We hang with him for several hours. We tell him we're just passing through town and staying with friends but need a hook up. He tells us he may be at a particular place off Seventh Street tomorrow around ten o'clock in the evening and he may be able to help.

We take it with a grain of salt, but we decide to show up anyway. The next night, there we are at a chicken joint off Seventh. By a quarter to eleven, we're starting to think he's a no-show. Killing time in a fast food place without a smartphone turns out to be excruciating.

Finally, he shows up. He's looking rougher than last night and we figure he's what the cops call "dope sick." We're going to a house where he knows a guy.

We feel like we're blending in at this point but we're still on alert like we're walking through a bad part of town. We make our way past a warehouse and some rinky-dink, rundown houses. We take a side street and we end up in front of a house with a sagging porch, peeling paint, and windows with black-out curtains.

Red's been talking this whole time but we've barely paid attention. The guy here is a friend of a friend and lets you hang out. "Just be cool," he says. He knocks and a tall, skinny black guy lets us in. We close the door behind us and make a sound like we're locking it but we don't.

The place is dim and smells like body odor, urine, and the odd chemical-ish smell from cooking heroin. There's very little furniture, just a lot of milk crates and a couch. The only light is from a flat-screen TV in the den and a few candles. There's a hallway ahead. A girl with dirty blonde hair walks down it shambling like a zombie. She turns off into another room. We hear a kid's voice down the hall. What the hell?

We stand like idiots in the hallway—the den is to the right—and we try to commit the place to memory without making eye contact with anyone. We've seen a lot of things with this project. We've spent nights out talking to people living on the street, gathering evidence for stories. But the squalor of it all is just overwhelming.

After what seems like too long, red is back. He tells us that we can go back with him and we'll split a quarter gram. Where's the cash?

At this point, we decide. If this exercise had any point it's been accomplished. It is time for us to go. We beg off, telling them we don't have the cash. The skinny tall black guy and another guy in a UK shirt with a barrel chest and arms to match step forward, menacing. We're out the door and down the sidewalk as quick as we can without running. We hear some loud voices behind us but we can't understand what they're saying.

People make bad choices but no one chooses to live like that. Yes, they made a bad choice at some point, and some of them are beyond saving. But not all of them. Like Eric said, you have to try.

There is a real villain here and it's not some street junkies or housewives hooked on pills. There's someone behind this opioid crisis that has been perpetrated on America.

7

Among the Culprits

Almost heaven, West Virginia
Blue Ridge Mountains, Shenandoah River
Life is old there, older than the trees
Younger than the mountains, blowing like a breeze
- "Take Me Home, Country Roads"

Crossing the border from eastern Kentucky, there's a sign on the interstate welcoming visitors to West Virginia. "Wild and Wonderful" it says proudly, and both the people and the natural beauty live up to the boast.

From the Blue Ridge Mountains to the Shenandoah River, this is gorgeous country. The ancient forests of sycamore and Norway maples, the winding streams and flowing waters, the dramatic rises and rock formations are all breathtaking. If you've never been here, you might picture it as some kind of post-industrial wasteland, picked clean by the coal companies. But these woods and mountains live up to the promise in the song.

At the little farmhouse we're renting, the wildlife is almost overwhelming. Raccoons are as fearless as city pigeons and big as dogs. It seems as if there are more deer in the yard every evening than people on the streets of some of the nearby towns. Something may have to be done about the overabundance of woodpeckers.

It's the middle of the week and we're driving along a winding mountain road. There don't seem to be any straightaways that last more than a quarter mile or so and we have fun taking the curves hard.

We pass Harts K-8 School and kids are playing at recess. We're surrounded by seven to nine hundred foot elevation rises and it feels cozy. In the small towns we pass through and on the outskirts, it's as common to see people getting around on ATVs and dirt-bikes as trucks. John Denver was right. Almost heaven.

Almost, if not for the soul-crushing poverty, the opioid abuse rates that now exceed 50 percent in parts of the state, and the never-ending advertisements for drug rehab clinics. Entire towns now seem populated almost entirely by drug-addicted zombies. In West Huntington, population 48,000, opioid-addicted prostitutes hit the streets on a weekday before the sun is even down, plying their trade on the streets within sight of children playing ball in a parking lot. But that's why we're here. We're here to see the good and the bad, in equal, unalloyed measure.

It seems like every little bridge and stretch of road is named in honor of a local boy who died a soldier. Overwhelmingly the honored dead are the lower enlisted ranks, with a few junior officers here and there. Appalachians and Southerners are invariably the first to answer when their country calls them to war, no matter how noble or pointless that war is. When Virginia Governor Jim Webb wrote his homage to the Scots-Irish, he titled it "Born Fighting," a nod to their spirit that features a natural patriotism and orneriness.

* * *

We take Old Logan Road and it puts us alongside the Guyandotte River. US Highway 119 would have been much faster but there's no substitute for the view we're getting. We drive along the narrow road through Mitchell Heights and its charming, clapboard houses. Old couples and families are sitting in rocking chairs on their porches enjoying the spring morning.

Right here in Logan, West Virginia we're in the nexus of several counties, where pharmaceutical companies and wholesalers have been pumping in pills by the tens of millions in the last decade. Logan isn't the hardest-hit area in terms of opioid abuse, but it's central to several of them. And even where things aren't downright awful, they are still bad.

Logan is coal country through and through. The entire economy is built on it. Logan County holds a special place in coal mining lore and the hearts of generations of coal miners. In 1921, it was the epicenter of the Battle of Blair Mountain, the largest armed uprising in American history since the Civil War. It was part of the Coal Wars. This part of American history isn't taught much outside of this part of the country.

The Coal Wars were a series of early twentieth century labor disputes that culminated in armed confrontation in Logan County. For five days in the late summer of 1921, about ten thousand armed coal miners confronted three thousand strikebreaker lawmen and "gun thugs" backed by the coal companies, who were fighting attempts by the miners to unionize their part of the state. More than a million rounds were fired, according to accounts, and as many as one hundred people died in the confrontation. The miners lost, but saw some concessions later on in working conditions.

Flash forward about eighty to ninety years, and all that cavalier and trendy green talk about shutting down "dirty coal" had real-world consequences. The region shed jobs rapidly under the combined pressure of environmental policies and cheap coal from overseas. Today, the town is a shell of what it was just a few decades ago.

Nearby Williamson, West Virginia lies in Mingo County. Over the past decade, out-of-state drug companies have shipped 20.8 million prescription painkillers to two pharmacies there. They lie only four blocks apart. That West Virginia town has just 2,900 residents.

Regional drug wholesalers Miami-Luken and H.D. Smith shipped some 10.2 million hydrocodone and 10.6 million oxycodone pills to just two area pharmacies—Tug Valley Pharmacy and Hurley Drug in Williamson—between 2006 and 2016, according to Congressional records.

Miami-Luken, based in Springboro, Ohio had dealings like this all over. It was the main wholesaler for a now-closed Save-Rite pharmacy located in the town of Kermit in Mingo County. They sent 5.7 million hydrocodone and oxycodone pills to outlets in Mingo County between 2005 and 2011.

For context, Kermit's population as of 2010 was about four hundred. The county seat, Williamson, has a population of about three thousand.

This is sadly not the worst of it. Just last year, according to the *West Virginia Gazette-Mail*, under increasing pressure from the US House Energy and Commerce Committee, Cardinal Health Executive Chairman George Barrett expressed regret that the drug company didn't do more to stop high-volume shipments of opioids to Family Discount Pharmacy in Mount Gay, Logan County and Hurley Drug in Mingo County in the early 2010s.

"With the benefit of hindsight, I wish we had moved faster and asked a different set of questions. I am deeply sorry we did not," Barrett told the committee back in May 2018. The drug wholesaler admitted it supplied Family Discount Pharmacy, in Mount Gay, with 6.5 million doses of hydrocodone and oxycodone between 2008 and 2012. That's 3,561 painkillers a day to a single pharmacy in rural Logan County. The panel also raised questions about Cardinal Health's hydrocodone shipments to Hurley Drug pharmacy in Williamson.

In his prepared remarks, Barrett said the company has taken steps that would have blocked questionable orders from such pharmacies, including bolstering its anti-diversion program.

Cardinal Health hasn't delivered opioids to Family Discount Pharmacy since 2012, or to Hurley Drug since 2014, according to

Barrett, but that hasn't slowed those two pharmacies. Neither the Drug Enforcement Administration nor the West Virginia Board of Pharmacy sanctioned Family Discount or Hurley Drug.

Both pharmacies are still dispensing prescription opioids and other controlled substances that they now obtain from other suppliers.

It was these kinds of half-measures and public hearings that, admittedly, did seem to slow prescription rates down some. But that only started a new wave of overdoses in West Virginia when heroin flooded the market, brought in from places like Detroit and Cincinnati.

A second wave of drug overdoses took off in the mid-2010s, as drug dealers took advantage of a new population of opioid users who either lost access to painkillers or simply sought a better, cheaper high. And now this southwestern area of West Virginia, much like the rest of the state, is in the middle of a third wave, as fentanyl offers an even more potent and cheaper, but deadlier, alternative to heroin.

What locals call "town critters" wander aimlessly about, searching for their next high. What locals call "fashion girls" make driving a little dangerous, because they're walking into the street trying to get the attention of potential customers.

Just up the road, in Kenova, West Virginia, on the same day we're in Logan, police arrested a woman who was allegedly selling drugs with a nine-year-old in the back of the vehicle. Police say that Cayla Watts, thirty, of Huntington had her nine-year-old child in the back seat of the car as she attempted to sell about $2,000 worth of fentanyl-laced heroin and crystal meth. It's heart-breaking to see this kind of misery amidst all this natural beauty.

Everyone points the finger at everyone else for why this is. One group says it's Big Pharma. Pharmacists say it's doctors who are irresponsible. Doctors blame bad information and/or patient abuse. Everyone involved finds a way to absolve themselves, mostly by pointing the finger at addicts. It's a classic display of victim blaming. And while for decades Big Pharma's lawyers and lobbyists in

Congress, AMA and the FDA, paved a superhighway for their flood of prescriptions, the matter has only gotten more complicated and ugly, with state lawmakers and trial lawyers in the last decade dog piling after seeing blood money in the water in the form of class action lawsuits—the goals of which often are far less based on justice or restoration and more on opportunism and avarice.

The truth is, ultimately, that they are all correct. No one has clean hands in this. That's something we're learning as we go on. This crisis is so difficult in part because it's full of seeming contradictions. No, physical addiction is not a moral failing, but until an addict takes personal responsibility, they don't have any real hope of getting and staying clean. No, physicians aren't responsible if legal drugs have negative impacts on patients, but the physician's name is on the prescription that ends up getting high school girls hooked on dope. Pharmacists may not be morally culpable if prescriptions are written with no medical purpose, but when they are selling millions of pills a year, they have to see past their bottom line and realize something is wrong. These inconsistencies keep us up at night.

So we figure we'll take it slow, and examine it from one perspective at a time. Since we're here in Logan, we plan to drop in at a small independent pharmacy that made headlines ten years ago under different ownership.

Note: The Family Discount Pharmacy in Logan proper is wholly unrelated to the Family Discount Pharmacy in Mount Gay, mentioned above.

Family Discount Pharmacy in Logan is located off the main road on a street surrounded by several auto service businesses, a carpet store, and a gas station. Beyond the main street, we're surrounded on all sides by steep mountain tops that rise seven or eight hundred feet above the town's base elevation.

Inside, we meet Ed Thornhill, RPH. He's a stocky man in a West Virginia University golf shirt, with receding grey hair, a matching moustache, blue eyes, and a Smith & Wesson .38 Airweight on his hip. He keeps a Kimber .45 under the counter for more serious problems. In 2013 an addict with a sawed-off shotgun created a hostage standoff that drew in the DEA and FBI. No one was hurt even though the perpetrator told Thornhill he just wanted to get high and die. Thornhill points out the repainted and repaired areas from where the addict fired off warning shots with the shotgun inside the pharmacy.

Thornhill is one of the good guys. He's got one of the cleanest pharmacy records in the state. He admits that the West Virginia Board of Pharmacy is reactive and lazy, but he's had more complaints for not filling opioid prescriptions than for filling too generously.

Funny thing about this area, it's easier to find the heroes than the villains in this ugly saga, even though the good guys are outnumbered like the Spartans at Thermopylae.

"For starters, when it comes to the reduction in the amount of prescribed opioids, I think they're maybe down a little nationally but nowhere near what the DEA and CDC tell you," Thornhill complains, clearly frustrated. "Come on, the government fudges the numbers on pretty much everything. They can shade things down when it's to their benefit and they can shade things up when it's to their benefit. That's on everything from crime to immigration, so you think they can't do the same with prescription numbers?"

He's not wrong. Officially, per capita prescribing grew exponentially around the turn of the century, so that by early 2010s more than 259 million prescriptions were written in the United States. That was the peak in 2013. According to the CDC, it's about 190 million now.

But there's a lot of wiggle room here. There are changes in the strength and duration of the medications prescribed. There are changes to how the CDC measures prescriptions and changes to the CDC's definition of an "opioid prescription." There are changes to the number of pills dispensed from wholesalers as the biggest pharmacies switched from receiving product from wholesalers to the actual manufacturers. Getting good data about the distribution of opiates is impossible, but one fact stands out. Drug companies aren't less profitable today than they were in 2013.

Here's a for-instance that doesn't require any idle speculation. In 2018, Huntington saw a roughly 40 percent decline in opioid overdoses. Some quickly seized on that statistic as proof of a marked decline in opioid use. But it wasn't. It turns out that it was almost entirely the result of expanded training in the use of naloxone, or Narcan, by first responders in the Huntington Fire Department, teachers, police, EMTs, and others. So there were more lives saved by Narcan, meaning fewer deaths, but that doesn't mean there's been any reduction in actual opioid use or opioid overdoses. They are just treating a symptom without curing the underlying disease.

"The biggest problem is the Board of Pharmacy says the practice of a pharmacist is a privilege and not a right," Thornhill says. "And therefore when the state gives you a license you have to fill every legal prescription put before you, and if I think I see red flags, I better be able to prove it, or it's a strike against me."

He also admits that there's the issue of staying in business, especially for independent shops like his that rely on personal relationships and extra services like free delivery. "I hate to admit it, but nobody can be a purist. This really gets me." He looks irritated. "Because other pharmacies aren't held to the standard the more ethical ones want to hold, we lose business. And for a place like this in a small town like this, if I don't fill a prescription that I am doubtful about but can't prove, I lose your business, and your sister, and your father-in-law and four or five other customers," Thornhill says. "It burns me up. I'd make it where we all have to meet the same standard, but there's no way you can really do that."

There have been some improvements, such as record sharing between West Virginia, Kentucky and Ohio, which makes it easier to prove red flags, but there's not enough pressure on pharmacies to make finding those red flags a priority. Consequently, he says, "The way you get busy is by being lenient. It's the difference between filling 200 prescriptions a week or a thousand."

"What you need is an active Board of Pharmacy that proactively sends out inspectors to check C2's and do it regularly instead of when the shit hits the fan," Thornhill says. C2's are prescriptions for Schedule II narcotics, which includes opiates.

While the prescription fillers are one place far more oversight is needed, the real problem, he says, are the prescribers. "If you take the doctor out of the equation, it would mostly stop," he says. "There's no one rule that will fix this and doctors aren't the only ones to blame, and most aren't to blame, but that's where the bottleneck is. And the professional board protects the bad ones."

* * *

Here's an old joke. What's the difference between a doctor and God? God doesn't think he's a doctor. Being an MD comes with a lot of responsibility, and consequently their judgment is afforded significant deference. This is why you only hear about them losing a license after the most egregious of behaviors. The presumption of "bad judgment" is the starting point for every mistake. And maybe in a lot of areas of medicine, given the high level of decision making going on, that should be the case. But the prescribing of addictive and deadly drugs might not be the proper area for this.

We combed through the records of some of the doctors in this region who have been arrested, jailed, or sanctioned, looking at everything from local police reports to small town local newspaper stories and, in the most prominent cases, national media coverage. The following is not comprehensive, but they are the worst of the worst, and it reads more like something out of a bonus content side story from *Nip and Tuck* than something you might title *Dr. Innocent Bad Judgment*.

Easily the most brazen in the last decade was Katherine Hoover.

From December 2002 to January 2010, she "wrote" more than 335,130 prescriptions for painkillers. That's about 130 per day, seven days a week, 365 days a year. She wrote more opioid prescriptions than any other doctor in West Virginia in the same time period.

Hoover worked with another doctor named William Ryckman in a clinic in Williamson. He was eventually charged with selling prescriptions to patients he never saw and did six months and more than $413,000 in fines. Hoover, now sixty-eight, simply closed the clinic and moved to the Bahamas, where she bought an island. In late 2018, *NBC News* scored an interview by phone with Hoover, where she basically said, "Sorry, not sorry."

"I was never charged or ever investigated because I didn't commit any crimes," Hoover told *NBC News*. "I prescribed narcotics to people in pain. I did everything I could to help people have a better life, which I told the FBI. Every prescription I wrote was justified for the person who had gotten it."

Federal prosecutors pursued her for a time, but she made it not worth their while. When you have island buying money for attorneys and a nation with very lax extradition, you can beat the system.

Here's the kicker—when Hoover opened her clinic in 2002, her medical license was suspended. She was only able to operate under the supervision of another doctor, the partner she would later abandon to face federal prosecution. Her offense at the time? She'd asked a seventeen-year-old patient to have sex with one of her sons. In exchange, she offered to waive the fees for her medical services.

Just combing through local news reports we see alleged patterns of behavior, money laundering, callous and reckless disregard for life. Not from street dealers, but licensed physicians.

According to a report from February 2018, about ten doctors at a place called Hope Clinic were charged with overprescribing pain pills in West Virginia and Virginia, in a case that left two patients dead. The ten doctors faced at the time a sixty-nine-count federal indictment for conspiracy to illegally distribute oxycodone and other controlled substances between 2010 and 2015. Hope Clinic wasn't a one-off—it operated four offices in West Virginia and Virginia.

And this case, the indictment alleges, wasn't a mere case of doctors with too heavy a hand with the prescription pad.

"Home-grown drug dealers hidden behind the veil of a doctor's lab coat, a medical degree and a prescription pad, are every bit as bad as the heroin dealers that flood into West Virginia," U.S. Attorney Michael Stuart said at a news conference. "We're not going to tolerate it."

Prosecutors allege that the owners and employees of Hope Clinic laundered the income by paying bonuses to physicians on the one hand, and bonuses to a patient-screening company that steered higher-risk patients to Hope Clinic on the other.

Sanjay Mehta, one of the ten physicians indicted, was charged in the two aforementioned patient deaths, going back to 2013.

Hope Clinic's owner, Dr. James H. Blume Jr. and his operational manager Mark T. Radcliffe were also charged with "maintaining drug-involved premises."

Prosecutors alleged that the pair operated Hope Clinic as a cash-only business and disregarded rules and regulations regarding patient care, including not requiring a physician referral for pain management treatment.

It took four years of investigating to bring charges against this ring despite two patients dying and mountains of evidence. The worst offenders list gets seedier and more degenerate. In 2016, Dr. Tressie Montene Duffy of Martinsburg, West Virginia lost her license, got a year and a day in jail and fines of $18,200. But that was four years after formal complaints surfaced accusing her of leaving signed prescription forms so that coworkers could issue Xanax, opioids, and valium. It eventually led to seven felonies for illegal distribution of oxycodone, but in the interim she continued to practice.

Thornhill tells us of one physician who was only removed from the board because he was arrested while high in Huntington. The doctor was stopped for speeding and found to have pounds of Oxy pills and crushed Adderall in his trunk. As the story has it, when police said "Sir, I need to see your driver's license," the MD responded, "I'm a doctor and I need to see your badge."

Most recently, in February 2019, a podiatrist from Boardman, Ohio who also practices in West Virginia was indicted for giving out pain pill prescriptions to some thirty patients.

Prosecutor Paul Gains and Ohio Attorney General Dave Yost announced that Dr. James Prommersberger, fifty-five, a Windham Court podiatrist, is facing seventy-nine felony counts of illegal processing of drug documents, trafficking in drugs, Medicaid fraud, and grand theft.

The podiatrist is accused of illegally prescribing the opioid medications hydrocodone and tramadol as well as the muscle relaxant carisoprodol to thirty patients between 2013 and 2017, according to the indictment. These charges stem from an investigation dating back to 2014, but as of this writing, Prommersberger is still practicing while awaiting trial. He has yet to have his medical license revoked.

"When the state comes down on a doctor like Prommesberger or even one not quite as obvious, those doctors just lawyer up and they get their board behind them," Thornhill says. "Some of these doctors have offices that look like there's a line for a Grateful Dead concert. Everyone knows which doctors are the ones doing this—they just don't have the fortitude to go after them."

Thornhill again stresses he's not blaming all doctors. Most don't practice like this—just the ones who want easy money. After all, you could take the time to see a patient every twenty minutes, really get to know their problems, and deal responsibly with any pain issues. "Or you could have two of your girls write out prescriptions ahead of time and see twenty patients an hour and bill for that," Thornhill says.

Thornhill has lobbied the West Virginia state government, the governor, his DEA drug task force, and his own Board of Pharmacy. There are some very practical changes that could be made. His favorite idea is to set up a commission with representatives from the board of licensing for law enforcement, doctors, pharmacists, and other health care professionals. It would examine the records of only the most red-flagged prescribers in the state. It wouldn't have the power to take a medical license, but would have the power after due process to say "You can practice somewhere else, but not West Virginia."

Additionally, to avoid any accusations of witch hunts, any commission member could veto an action by the commission. "You wouldn't have to take out all the doctors or even many," Thornhill says. "Just a handful. I was talking to Mike Smith at the Drug Task Force, and I said Mike, what if we could just get rid of the top ten opioid prescribers and make sure they couldn't practice in West Virginia, what difference would that make? He looked at the numbers and his eyes went wide."

We're about an hour away from Logan on the winding road back to the rented farmhouse when the implication of what he just said hits us. That means his friend on the drug task force has a list where they know who the biggest prescribers are, with an ability to cross-reference confidential complaints to the Board of Medicine, as well as their internal, classified investigative material. We can look at raw prescription rates for past years—they know who is throwing up the worst red flags.

Certainly the doctors and pharmacists that peddle opiates are on the front lines when it comes to blame, because they are the gatekeepers for legal, prescription opioids. But they're not the kingpins in this crisis any more than local street drug dealers are in the illicit black-market drug trade. Guilty, for sure, but they're still the small fish.

8

Too Close to Home

Authors' Note: The following story involves an attempted suicide by overdose of a thirteen-year-old girl. Names and identifying details have been changed to protect her identity and the identities of sources working in the hospital who spoke on condition of anonymity. The following is an account of the personal incident that occurred during the research for this book to one of the authors.

This is not the story I was expecting to tell. This is not a story I was wanting to tell. This is, though, a story that has to be told.

This story begins with the genesis of the opioid epidemic in rural and working-class America. But you know that if you've made it to this chapter. This particular story begins with a blood-chilling text message sent from a daughter to a mother:

"Mom, I did something bad. Get home. Get some activated charcoal."

I should probably back up a bit.

I had been in the Eastern Kentucky and West Virginia area for weeks. It's absolutely gorgeous country and I hope I've done justice in describing it so far. The white fence horse farms, the rolling hills and mountains, the deep, old forests and countless rivers—I'm a Southerner and a Texan by temperament and by choice, but I could see the draw of moving to this part of the country.

But it's a country as troubled as it is beautiful, awash in poverty, shuttered coal mines, and the plague of drug addiction and despair.

I could probably write this entire book based on the stories of substance abuse, addiction, death and destruction I see just in this area. It's everywhere. I can't even escape these tales in my off hours. I sit at a coffee shop and make small talk for five minutes, and I mention why I'm in town and within moments I'm hearing the story of another overdose. Another family member dead or in jail from pills or heroin or some other chemical garbage injected, snorted, or smoked.

Ordinary people I meet when I'm off-the-clock—bartenders and waiters, bookstore clerks and the guys changing the oil in my car— I'm not exaggerating when I tell you that every one of them has a story of tragedy and loss stemming from the poison that runs through these hills and hollows. Each is convinced that their little corner of West Virginia or Kentucky is ground zero for the opioid plague, and in a way they're right. It doesn't take much to get them to talk about the painful, intimate experiences they've survived. Every one of them has a story that needs to be told.

Hell, this book could entirely be a series of first-person accounts of how opioid addiction wrecked their lives, took away family members, ravaged their communities, and stole their children. It's everywhere here.

Sometimes when I'm making small talk, when I just need a break from it all, I tell people I'm writing a book on the history of bluegrass music. I don't even know much about bluegrass, though I'm learning. But that's okay, because it never draws out the conversation the way a mention of hillbilly heroin does.

That willingness to talk is what has built my network of sources. I've gotten to know a lot of these people more closely than the typical "parachute in" journalist. Some are just random folks I've met, but the bulk of them work in and around this epidemic in all manner of roles. Some are police and drug agents, on the frontline in the battle against this monster. Many are in the health care and rehabilitation/recovery field. A number are interventionists and counselors—many of them are recovered addicts themselves. Many others are advocates and activists, trying to get this crisis the attention and funding it needs in the face of a public and politicians who still view opioid addiction as a moral failing of the dependent user, rather than the natural and predictable result of decades of Big Pharma flooding working-class, predominantly White communities with a blizzard of prescriptions and a tidal wave of pills.

* * *

So it was on a warm and clear Wednesday evening in April in Boyd County, Kentucky, that one of our sources, Lauren, was having drinks and cooking out with her girlfriends and some of their daughters. They were enjoying themselves at Lauren's friend's house, a mile away but in the same neighborhood where Lauren lives. They were doing a few shots of New Amsterdam peach vodka in the little red solo shot cups.

A little background on Lauren. She's an outspoken advocate in the community for more rehabilitation services and a bit of a political gadfly. She's lost several family members to drugs and alcohol. Before her divorce she had to deal with her ex-husband attempting suicide three separate times using opioids.

In short, this is a woman who is aware of the signs of addiction as well as depression, and is very protective of her daughters, as a result. The oldest is eighteen and already in college. Her youngest, Sarah, is thirteen and wants to be a forensic psychologist.

As with most of the sources I've developed in the time I've been working on this project, I text Lauren semi-regularly, and she sends me updates on the too frequent headlines in her neck of the woods relevant to my interests.

Meanwhile, I was about an hour east of Boyd County in Charleston, West Virginia. I'd been camped there for a while, talking to lawyers and state legislators, getting a feel of the local ground.

Around the time that Lauren was having some drinks and food with her friends and Sarah was home alone, I was taking a break from the world of the opioid plague. I was on a group call with some friends, unwinding and talking about nothing. But I should have known that while I can take a night off, the opioid crisis doesn't.

"We were just having a good time, me and my little coven," Lauren told me later. "Normally Sarah would come with me because she's friends with the other ladies' daughters, but she said she wanted to stay home."

Lauren and her girlfriends watched the sun go down, and it got a little chilly. The peach vodka warmed them inside as much as the camaraderie.

At 8:13 p.m., Lauren got the text from Sarah:

"Mom, I did something bad. Get home. Get some activated charcoal."

Lauren dropped her phone. She picked it up again and read it again, not wanting to believe what she knew it meant.

As her friends hustled Lauren to the car, another text came in.

"Don't call 911. They'll want to commit me."

Lauren was on the phone to the family doctor, who advised her to take Sarah to the emergency room. When Lauren crashed through the door to her house, she found Sarah sitting on the couch, rocking and breathing heavy.

Only Sarah will ever know for sure if she really wanted to commit suicide or if it was a cry for help, which is not uncommon. But there are a few facts to consider.

Suicidal people deal with a struggle that part of them wants to die but part of them wants to live. The survival instinct is hard-wired into human beings. Sometimes people make a half-hearted attempt at suicide for attention, but more often they only go halfway through on an attempt because they're fighting their better nature. Remember, all twenty-nine people who have survived a suicide attempt by jumping off San Francisco's Golden Gate Bridge said they regretted their decision as soon as they jumped.

At some point after she took an overdose of pills, long enough for them to start to metabolize but before they were fully in her system, she made herself vomit. And that's when she texted her mother.

An opioid overdose doesn't kill immediately. The most basic avenue of death from one is that breathing is slowed, and eventually stopped. That's basically what kills you. But if this is a book about the opioid crisis, I'd be remiss not to explain exactly what happens with an overdose, paraphrasing Anthony Morocco, ER doctor at Sharp Memorial Hospital in San Diego, California:

The first thing that happens when you take an opioid by whatever delivery means is that it spreads throughout your body via the bloodstream. That opioid-rich blood plugs into the system of opioid receptors all over your body. That feeling of euphoria users describe comes when it hits the brain receptors. That happens once those opioid molecules cross the blood-brain barrier, where they enter a section of the brain at the center of your reward circuitry called the nucleus accumbens. That's where dopamine is produced. There, the drug latches onto cells called GABAergic neurons. Normally the GABA serves as a block to make sure dopamine doesn't overflow, but opioid molecules knock that barrier down and let dopamine spill over into the bloodstream, creating the euphoria users crave.

Meanwhile, physically, breathing slows. Opioids affect the systems that control both sleep and breathing. At the base of your brain lies a respiratory control center that drives respiration, reacting to the level of carbon dioxide and oxygen in your blood to spur you to breathe. During an overdose, the slowed breathing that occurs with opioid ingestion of any kind becomes dangerously slow, potentially leading to a complete cessation of breath.

Then the heart rate slows as the opioid suppresses neurological signals. The oxygen level falls low enough that the heart cannot beat properly and begins having abnormal rhythms. At this point some overdose patients have sudden cardiac arrest.

The whole body then begins to shut down. Because there is an overwhelming amount of opioid in the brain, the body stops receiving the correct signals at all to breathe. At this point the lungs and heart are barely working. Brain damage follows from the proper lack of oxygen. Permanent brain damage sets in after four minutes of oxygen deprivation in most situations.

Lauren knows all too well the signs to look for in a potential overdose. Loss of consciousness, lack of response to outside stimulus, the shallow and erratic breathing, skin turning a bluish purple, snore-like gurgling noises, clammy skin, and erratic pulse.

Lauren drove Sarah to the emergency room in Boyd County. The work of the next two hours would not be about why or how, but simply getting Sarah stable. Sarah has a complicated health history. She's had a host of problems up to and including bone cancer. An overdose of opioids can and will kill a healthy adult without intervention. For an adolescent with a compromised immune system and hypertension? There was a reason they monitored Sarah so closely even after they were sure she was stable.

For two hours, with Sarah nodding in and out of consciousness, doctors kept a close eye on her blood pressure, her breathing, and her heart rate. Biting her own nails, Lauren alternated between holding her daughter's hand and slipping outside for a stolen moment to smoke a Marlboro Light in the parking lot.

Somewhere in the middle of that two hours, Lauren texted me, among other close contacts, *"My kid overdosed."*

I wouldn't see the message for another hour. But around a quarter after eleven, the attending physician declared that Sarah was stable enough to transport to the Pediatric Intensive Care Unit at Cabell Huntington Hospital for care and observation. It was about thirty minutes away.

* * *

Lauren followed the ambulance through the night along Interstate 64, knuckles white on the steering wheel. I was on the same interstate coming west from Charleston. We'd texted and I'd gotten the info.

Lauren isn't just a source. She's a mother and an advocate and one more human being whose life has been ravaged by the opioid plague. In any other context of traditional journalism, editors would tell me I was getting too close to the story. But so what? How can you tell the story if you're not that close? All attempts at telling stories are, at best, like Plato's shadows on the cave wall. If being a shoulder to cry on or holding a little girl's hand while her mother fills out insurance paperwork hurts the story, then it's the story that should suffer. To be honest, I don't think it does.

I pulled into emergency parking maybe twenty minutes after Sarah was admitted to the PICU on the fifth floor. It was thirty minutes after midnight. I went in through the ER because I didn't know where else to go.

Huntington, as you read earlier, is an attractive little town of 49,000 on the banks of the Ohio River, with a homicide rate as high as Detroit's. It's stricken by a cruel poverty that comes in equal measures from hopelessness and lack of purpose. I'm walking through the night which has gotten considerably colder. The red light from the hospital EMERGENCY sign casts an eerie glow on the sidewalk. On this early Thursday morning, the waiting room at the ER is half full.

At this point I'm anxious and nervous because I haven't had any update since I tore out of my hotel room and into the night along I-64. What I do know is that Lauren's friends are taking care of Lauren's older daughter so that she doesn't have to be there, and that Sarah's father, whom Lauren divorced a year ago, hasn't returned the voice mail that she left more than three hours before.

I have to wait about ten minutes for the system to update to even show Sarah as a patient. I'm from a medical family so I know getting impatient with the charge nurse gains you nothing and risks a lot. I wait as patiently as I can. Lauren texts to tell me that when I can sign in, to sign in as an uncle since they only allow family into the Pediatric Intensive Care Unit. Sure, why not? This definitely seems like one of those situations where God will let the white lie slide in service to the greater good.

Yellow visitor pass in hand, I make my way up to PICU. Lauren is in the hallway outside. They're still getting Sarah settled into her room and even her mother isn't allowed back, yet. Lauren, naturally, looks haggard and disheveled. She's wearing her dad's old Army coat over the t-shirt and jeans she was cooking out in just hours before. I give her a hug and I can tell that she'd like nothing more than to collapse. Never underestimate a mother's strength when it comes to looking after her young. Lauren would still be standing long after I'd collapsed if they kept us out here long enough.

Ava, a PICU nurse, brings us back to Sarah's room. Every room is dark but occupied. In the hallway, because it's the night shift, cleaning crews are at work. Ava's a small woman, a little mousy, dressed in dark green scrubs and her dark hair in a ponytail, but she knows her stuff. She's seen too many such cases. She does her best to present a calm, knowing demeanor, the kind that makes upset parents feel safe despite their child being here.

We enter the room and it's the first time I've seen Sarah. She's a little pale and her blonde hair is pulled back. She's in and out of consciousness, though she does acknowledge her mom's presence before she nods off again.

I look at her and I see every man's daughter. I see my daughter. This girl is thirteen. She's taken so many advanced placement classes she is set to graduate high school at age sixteen. She should be hanging out with her friends, giggling over boys or experimenting with makeup. She has the whole world and her whole life in front of her. Instead she's in hospital pajamas with an IV in her arm, a depressed heart rate, elevated blood pressure, and a dedicated nurse who is here to maintain one-to-one observation all night because of her suicide attempt.

Her mother is stoically answering insurance questions. I'm wiping away tears. I don't know what brought her to this. I don't know how she got access to the pills. I don't even think I was aware yet that it was a suicide attempt and not an accidental overdose. All I see is that except by the grace of God and immediate medical care, this is another future that could have been erased.

"Is there anything she's expressed concern or depression over?" Ava asks as nicely as she can. Lauren explains that three months ago, her grandfather with whom she was close died in Florida. Last year her father, an addict and an alcoholic, divorced her mother and went to live with a second family he maintained. Sarah's bone cancer, while in remission, took her out of school much of the previous year and she's been homeschooled since. She's still maintained her circle of friends but it shrunk.

I'm on the outside and none of what she mentions would seem to add up to suicide-levels of depression, but one thing I've learned is that depression isn't necessarily event-driven. It's not always caused by some great tragedy in your life, but rather chemical imbalances in the brain that can affect people who appear to have perfect lives and few worries.

"Where did she get the pills," I keep asking myself.

Ironically, the part of the story I was working on before all this happened was about how easy it still is, despite state and federal curbs, to get prescriptions for all manner of opioids. All that the crackdown has done is add a few steps that doctors and drug-seekers have to go through and then it's back to business as usual. Between that and what pharmacists have told me about how the numbers of reported prescriptions can be juked by the CDC and Department of Health and Human Services, it's not hard to see how there are plenty of illicit pills out there on the streets.

Lauren steps outside to have another cigarette—who can blame her—and I stay and talk to Ava. She agrees to speak to me on the record but not using her name because of hospital policy.

Sarah is fortunate, she tells me, because of her insurance and because a suicide attempt by a minor comes with a mandatory observation hold. She's seen too many adolescents and teens who come in for overdoses and are released within hours.

"If they have a good family, then their family will try to get them treatment and try to make sure they don't get access to drugs again," Ava says. "But so many of these kids are being raised by their grandparents because their parents are either in jail or don't have custody of their kids because of their own substance abuse or because of court orders."

"Those kids are back out on the street in hours sometimes, and end up going right back to their friends or dealers and using again," she says. "It's especially dangerous when they've been given naloxone (Narcan), because they end up taking higher doses to try to get that high and they overdose again."

I ask Ava how often they have kids through PICU for drug overdoses. Her eyes look a little haunted, but she also looks at me like I asked the dumbest question in the world. "All the time," she says.

• • •

The nurses bring linens for Lauren to sleep in the room with Sarah. It's somewhere around three o'clock in the morning, and Sarah hasn't awakened since we first arrived. She looks like an angel, of course. Every girl at that age is beautiful and has the potential of an unalloyed lifetime in them. Yet Sarah's father hasn't returned the voice mail telling him his daughter nearly overdosed and is in the hospital. Lauren's friends are making sure her other daughter is okay.

"Are you going to have her see the counselor tomorrow?" I ask. It's part of the hospital's program for youths with attempted suicides. It's not mandatory and requires parental permission.

"No. I'm going to sign her out tomorrow soon as they let me," she tells me. She has a network of counselors and interventionists she works with fighting the opioid plague in her corner of Boyd County, Kentucky, but it's a fight that it seems everyone is losing.

Overdose deaths are declining, but overdoses are on the rise. The easy and widespread availability of Narcan saves lives but it masks the toll of use, and gives politicians artificial numbers to brag about. The CDC is projecting that the next big health crisis in this area will be HIV and Hepatitis—a combination of the needle sharing addicts engage in and the prostitution that accompanies heroin users.

I head back to my hotel. I text Lauren the next evening at 7:59 p.m. I ask her if they're home like she planned. They're still in the PICU, but hoping that Sarah will be transferred to the pediatrics unit later that night. Lauren thinks they'll be home by Friday now.

I want to ask her if she know where her daughter got the pills, or if she's talked more about why she made such a stupid decision. I want to, but I can't. Partly because I don't want to live up to the ghoulish journalist stereotype. And partly because it doesn't matter, does it? As to the why, that's something for her and Sarah and a therapist to work out among themselves. And as to the where she got the pills, I already know where. Around here, you don't have to look hard. The pills, the heroin, and everything else is there for the taking. The drug task forces and narcotics raids? They only scratch the surface.

Then comes a text I didn't expect. Lauren's family, like so many others in this corner of Appalachia, goes back generations to the eighteenth century. Her roots and her family are tied to this soil as surely as the bluegrass in the fields and hollows. She's been fighting to get people in power in her small town to put more resources into rehabilitation and intervention, because she sees this as an existential threat to her people, her piece of Appalachia. This woman is a fighter.

Or she was. *"We've decided to leave. I'm moving as soon as the house sells."*

So I shed a tear for the second time. The pills didn't kill her or her daughter. But they killed a little piece of their America.

9
Doctor Feelgood

Let's play the game of pills. Specifically, let's look at how easy is it to get prescription opioids in an America that is just starting to wake up to the plague that has descended on this land.

This will be a long way around but everything that follows leads to the completion of this game. Let's also look at how the medical community has been behaving since states and the federal authorities have started taking a closer look at the opioid plague and medical practices.

By now you've gotten the point that we're neck-deep in an opioid crisis that goes back at least to the 1990s, is killing hundreds of Americans every day, and shows no signs of stopping.

You've learned that, at least according to how the US Centers for Disease Control and Prevention mark it, the number of opioid and opiate prescriptions peaked around 2013.

Let's assume for this exercise that the CDC figures are broadly correct and that there has been a decline in the number of opioid prescriptions since 2013. The decline is attributed to a number of factors. First, there is the broader sharing of prescription and patient databases, and stricter state and federal guidelines on the prescription of narcotics.

Specifically, in response to the growing opioid crisis among youths and adults, many states adopted prescribing guidelines for primary care physicians from the CDC and passed laws and regulations to reduce the supply of unused, misused, and diverted prescriptions. Primary care physicians, for instance, have restrictions on the number of days of pain medication they can prescribe for acute pain in most states now. Many states require or encourage doctors to review state prescription databases to see if the patient is doctor shopping, and many require drug testing before a patient can be prescribed opioids.

Opioid prescribing guidelines and recommendations, as well as provider resources, vary by state. But basically, if you go to your doctor for acute pain like a pulled muscle, if he does prescribe some kind of Schedule II narcotic, you'll only get a three to five-day supply, and you'll have to visit them again for a refill. It can't be just called into the pharmacy. These physicians are then encouraged to refer you to a pain management clinic or other alternative treatment should your situation prove chronic.

Another factor in the decline of prescriptions, at least according to doctors, is the increased scrutiny and prosecution of offending prescribers by state and federal authorities. And it is undeniable that law enforcement prosecution largely shut down the old Wild West pill mills in places like Florida and Ohio over the past decade. How bad was it? We turned to one of the pill mill cowboys.

Joe Turner is a solidly built man of almost forty from Bourbon County, Kentucky, just a little northeast of Lexington. If anyone ever embodied the concept of the duality of man in the Robert Louis Stevenson "Jekyll and Hyde" sense, it's Joe Turner.

He was raised a Roman Catholic and was an Eagle Scout. He was also born into a motorcycle club, the James Gang, where his father was president. Both his parents were alcoholics. When he was just a boy he saw his mother shoot his stepfather. He lived.

"I started drinking when I was eight-year-old so I could be like my dad," Turner tells us. "I would drink his Oyster Bourbon every time he passed out. Which was about every night. I started smoking pot when I was twelve."

When his father left home, at least in part because someone blew up the bikers' clubhouse, Turner turned his need for approval to his stepfather. "When I turned sixteen my stepfather thought I would be a good drug runner since I couldn't go to jail. So I had money, drugs and women at age sixteen. I thought I'd hit the promised land," he says.

Around this time he went from drug runner to drug addict. He was prescribed Lortab, an opioid pain reliever, after a car accident when he was eighteen.

"When I was prescribed pain pills," he says, "I fell in love."

Despite all the distractions, extracurriculars, and his addiction, Turner was a high-functioning addict. At the same time he got his Eagle Scout badge, finished high school and went to college. He even got married to his high school sweetheart.

Turner was a master electrician and got a degree in sound engineering but he couldn't keep a job because he couldn't pass a drug test. He had to content himself wiring houses with his stepfather and later getting a job as a master electrician with Lexmark.

In 2007-2008, when the housing crisis hit, he was laid off. Joe the Hillbilly Heroin Outlaw didn't see a problem, he saw an opportunity.

"I conned a bank into loans to buy two vans and I paid people to ride to Florida non-stop. That was when one person on the Florida-Kentucky pipeline could get 150 Percocet 15s, 120 Xanax bars and 200 Percocet 30s in one trip for just $700. Ten to twelve people to a van, two vans, running all the time," Turner tells us. He sounds almost like a veteran commodities trader. In a way he was. He brought in OxyContin and every other opioid and opiate he could get.

Turner was clearing around $20,000 a month after all expenses. "I had a nice house, two cars, a wife and kid—and all I was doing was organizing the runs, selling what they brought back and drinking and doing pills all the time," Turner said.

When Florida authorities cracked down on the pill mills, Turner never recovered. "We tried Tennessee and North Carolina but we couldn't keep the connections. Nothing was like Florida before the crackdown," he says. "I started stealing from everyone. I went from being a big-time drug runner to being a kick-in artist. I stole my mother's debit card, stole everything I could."

Turner's story illustrates one side of the impact of the crackdown. And while it's a story for another time, his also has a happy ending. After a series of arrests and rehab, he has become one of the leading national intervention experts in the country and runs an international recovery organization.

The Florida crackdown is a kind of limited success, getting rid of some of the most egregious over-prescribers and stemming a large scale inter-state drug trade. Results elsewhere are less clear cut. And many states continue to struggle with significant over-prescription and lackadaisical enforcement.

Across Kentucky, there are more than 19,000 professionals registered with the DEA to administer, prescribe, or store controlled drugs, in addition to pharmacies and clinics. They include oral surgeons, pain specialists, addiction-treatment specialists, emergency room physicians, pharmacists, veterinarians, and medical researchers.

Kentucky is among the top ten states with the highest prescribing rates. In 2017, Kentucky providers wrote 86.8 opioid prescriptions for every one hundred persons, compared to the average U.S. rate of 58.7 prescriptions. The 2017 prescribing rate, however, represents more than a 36 percent decrease from a peak of 137.0 opioid prescriptions per one hundred persons in 2011.

In 2017, there were 1,160 reported opioid-involved deaths in Kentucky—a rate of 27.9 deaths per one hundred thousand persons, compared to the average national rate of 14.6 deaths per one hundred thousand persons.

From 2011 to 2015, only twelve out of every one thousand doctors were disciplined for overprescribing narcotics in Kentucky. Around twenty of the state's physicians were charged as drug dealers in federal court. In 2017 just five medical professionals registered with the DEA to access controlled substances were arrested across

Kentucky.

Much more often, forty times last year, the DEA issued letters of admonition, ordering corrective steps, or more formal memorandums of agreement, which can involve federal oversight for months or years.

Now in fairness, it was only very recently that federal, state, and local law enforcement began sharing not only criminal intelligence, but also patient and prescription information. The creation of multijurisdictional narcotics task forces targeting both illicit suppliers and legal prescribers has borne fruit.

Tom Synan, chief of the Newtown Police Department and head of the Hamilton County Heroin Coalition, said the recent change in federal and inter-state cooperation has been a godsend for his force's efforts, and he hopes it signals a change in how law enforcement at all levels view the drug problem.

"Cops can be out there doing street buys and building cases all day long, meanwhile the pharmaceutical companies and doctors are pushing the pills out there legally and fentanyl is being mailed in from China," Synan tells us.

As a case in point of what he said they need more of, just a few weeks before we sat down with Synan in May 2019, the Appalachian area saw the biggest legal action of its kind. Federal prosecutors charged sixty physicians and pharmacists with illegally handing out and filling opioid prescriptions in a sweeping takedown. The defendant list includes thirty-one medical doctors, twenty-two licensed medical professionals, and seven owners, operators, or clinic employees.

According to the press release form the Justice Department, the operation by the Appalachian Regional Prescription Strike Force included more than three hundred investigators from jurisdictions in Kentucky, Ohio, Tennessee, Alabama, and West Virginia. The operation was revealing for just how blatantly and overtly some prescribers and pharmacists operate, even in light of the supposed crackdown. Accusations included, among other things, that doctors were trading drugs for sex, or giving prescriptions to Facebook friends without conducting even a rudimentary exam (much less that which is prescribed by state regulations). Astonishingly, some dentists were accused of pulling patients' teeth unnecessarily to justify writing prescriptions for pain pills. The scope of the investigation goes back almost three years.

Of the incidents that made up the justifications for the mass warrants and roundups, at least five patients, including a pregnant woman from Tennessee, died from overdoses. When all the allegedly illegal prescriptions were totaled up, prosecutors in the US Attorney's office told us they amounted to more than thirty-two million opioid pills in the hands of patients and traffickers.

The bulk of the charges in the round up in April 2019 are for the unlawful distribution of controlled substances. Authorities say those charged gave out about 350,000 improper prescriptions in Ohio, Kentucky, Tennessee, West Virginia, and Alabama to some 28,000 patients.

According to formal written statements and press releases we received from federal prosecutors, the medical specialties involved and the methods used to skirt laws and regulations varied widely. Those arrested include orthopedic surgeons, dentists, general practitioners, and nurse practitioners. But the outcomes of the schemes were always the same. Victims dependent or addicted to opioids received dangerous, illegal, and sometimes lethal amounts of opioids and opiates. The defendants stand accused of writing or filling prescriptions outside the course of medical practices and prescribing them despite having no legitimate medical reasons to do so.

In a written statement to the press, Assistant US Attorney General Brian Benczkowski said that "if so-called medical professionals are going to behave like drug dealers, we're going to treat them like drug dealers." J. Douglas Overbey, U.S. Attorney in the Eastern District of Tennessee, went further in his statement, saying the doctors arrested "are simply white-coated drug dealers."

Another silver lining in this particular operation is that for the first time in any kind of case like this, federal law enforcement is partnering with public health officials to help the patients of the health care providers that were arrested. They are the victims, even if they are often willing victims, of the alleged criminals. Without some recourse or help, their addiction will simply drive them to seek other unethical providers, or worse, turn to street alternatives like heroin and fentanyl.

In that same written statement, Benjamin Glassman, the U.S. Attorney for the Southern District of Ohio said authorities recognize that closing clinics and arresting those who ran them won't solve the addiction problems of the patients who received the prescriptions. In an effort to help, he said, a public health official will be stationed at every clinic affected by the arrests.

The hope is that "when these facilities are taken down, there are resources in place to give the best possible chance for those victims to get proper treatment," Glassman said.

Synan tells us that this part of the operation, in his opinion, is just as important as the busts. He echoes something I've heard from a number of voices in law enforcement: You can't arrest your way out of this crisis and you can't just punish addiction out of people.

"Some people obviously need to be behind bars but for so many it's more important we break that cycle of addiction. I'm not saying that as bleeding heart, I mean when we get people off the drugs and into jobs, then they are not committing property crime or prostitution or all the other crimes they commit to support their habit or because they can't hold down a job," he says. "That's just the practical reality."

In supplemental documents, federal prosecutors detailed some of the worst practices among those arrested. A physician in Dayton, Ohio, collected $5,000 a month in rent from a pharmacy located in his office, which provided pills after he signed prescriptions. Many of those arrested signed blank prescriptions and left them for their office staff to fill out when they were unavailable. A number of doctors allegedly handed out pills directly for cash payments, including to pregnant women. More broadly, doctors would send patients across state lines to see other general practitioners, or write prescriptions "five weeks every four," a scheme for skirting calendar differences to get around time regulations. Sometimes doctors worked the acute care to chronic pain management pipeline.

It may seem gratuitous or salacious, but it's important to develop a sense for how medical professionals have been operating in the last couple of years. Even after the opioid crisis started percolating up into the national consciousness, and after the initial crackdown on the worst actors, many medical professionals continued to write prescription after prescription, because it remains incredibly profitable, to this day.

So we're going to detail the names and allegations from the raid.

The following information came directly from the US Attorneys' offices involved in the May 2019 Appalachian roundup and detailed the charges at the time:

Dr. Ijaz Mahood, of Elizabethtown, Kentucky, was arrested and charged with conspiring with others to defraud Medicare, Tricare, Medicaid, Anthem, and other health programs through the use of fraudulent claims. Prosecutors allege that between 2015 and 2019, he ordered his non-physician staff to write them prescriptions for narcotics, leaving a blank, signed prescription pad for them to use.

Dentist Dr. Denver Tackett of McDowell, Kentucky was indicted for prescribing Oxycodone and hydrocodone at unreasonable rates, and—most shockingly—he was accused of pulling teeth out of six patients from 2016 to 2018 who had no need for such a dental procedure. He was also charged with Medicare and Medicaid fraud.

Dr. Mohammed A.H. Mazumder of Prestonsburg, Kentucky, and owner of Appalachian Primary Care, was likewise charged with having non-physician employees evaluate and write prescriptions for narcotics in his absence between 2015 and 2019. After thism his clinic would submit claims to Medicare and Medicaid pretending that Mazumder had provided the treatment and written the prescriptions.

Tanya Mentzer, an office manager at a family medical practice in Hoover, Alabama with no medical background, was charged with conspiring with a physician and a manager to illegally dispense controlled substances. The whole operation was a classic "pill mill, frequently providing dangerous, addictive, powerful opioid cocktails" federal prosecutors alleged.

At another family clinic in Hoover, Dr. Elizabeth Korcz and two employees ran another pill mill, operating past midnight and only accepted cash patients, a huge red flag. Prescriptions flowed out in unreasonable numbers and were written even during Korcz's frequent and long leaves of absence.

Dr. Marshall Plotka has a medical practice in Huntsville, Alabama. A criminal complaint accuses him of owning a house and making it available for the purpose of storing, distributing, and using illegal drugs including heroin, methamphetamine, cocaine, and marijuana. Women addicted to drugs were hired by Plotka as prostitutes and then recruited as patients. The complaint says Huntsville police made thirty-five calls for service at the house from October 2015 to April 2019, including an overdose in 2018 by one of Plotka's "patients."

Dr. Thomas Ballard III was arrested and accused of maintaining a drug-involved premises, as well as illegally distributing and dispensing controlled substances. The indictment also accused Ballard of seeking sexual favors in exchange for prescriptions.

And then there was Jeffrey Young, a nurse practitioner who was indicted for trading opioids for sex. Young, who called himself the "Rock Doc" was accused of writing prescriptions for half a million hydrocodone pills, 300,000 oxycodone pills and 1,500 fentanyl patches over the course of three years. Charged with Young were his supervising physicians Dr. Alexander Alperovich and Dr. Andrew Rudin.

That's not a comprehensive list of those arrested, but it does give insight into how both banal and seedy this whole business is, even among the white coats that are supposed to be our health care heroes.

We'd like to believe that the arrests for these reprobates and fifty-two of their colleagues was a major undertaking and had a big impact. It was a major blow through the medical community throughout Appalachia.

Completely independent of all this, we looked into exactly how opiates remained so readily available. During our time in Jasper, Alabama, we dropped in on what was a questionable looking pain management clinic just to inquire what it would take to become a patient. We were told at the time the price would be $300 up front, and we would have to provide referrals and charts from a primary care physician. After that for chronic pain treatment, it would be $200 a month.

The crackdown on prescribing and most of the regulations for Schedule II narcotics which include opioids has largely been on acute care situations; that is, people with recent surgeries or injuries. That's where the limit of three to five days' worth of pills in most states comes from. Refills require follow-up visits, and after that primary care physicians are urged to refer patients to pain management clinics which, in theory, will work out long-term plans for patients. The plans include physical therapy, non-narcotic alternative treatments/pain management, and, when necessary, long-term and monitored narcotic treatments.

In practice, investigators tell us, there are many unscrupulous operators who set up pain management clinics and operate similarly to the pill mills of previous years. They meet the letter of the law, perhaps, but not the spirit. They check the boxes, but the primary purpose is to provide narcotic prescriptions, not genuine alternative pain management.

And that's what we were curious about. What would it take to get a prescription for opioids, and how fast could we get a referral for pain management? What we didn't know while planning this or making the appointment with the doctor is that three days before we would see a primary care physician in Kentucky, the massive five-state federal roundup would happen.

The doctor we picked wasn't random. Nor did we intentionally seek out a provider that seemed shady or that one of our sources tipped us to as a "Doctor Feelgood." We simply went to the wellhead. We went to the physician who prescribed the most opioid pills in the state of Kentucky, according to the most current records gathered by ProPublica.

We think it's important to stress now that medical doctors do and should have broad leeway in judgment, and that what follows is not an accusation of any unethical or illegal behavior. It is simply a description of how the events unfolded.

The Monday after the raids we found ourselves in the waiting room of Dr. John Richard. It's a nicely decorated space, with a flat screen playing health care and nutrition educational shorts on loop, fresh flowers on the table, comfortable leather furniture, and new magazines. The office is located on the second floor of a center in a posh part of southwest Lexington, Kentucky, not far from upscale shopping and restaurants.

Dr. Richard is listed as the number one prescriber of hydrocodone-acetaminophen in the state of Kentucky, as ranked by Medicare claims, according to ProPublica. Note that the ranking by Medicare claims is the best measure for tracking prescription rates, because Medicare pays for one in four prescriptions nationally and there is no other national public record available to track prescriptions.

Of Dr. Richard's 3,358 patients using Medicare, 37 percent of them filled at least one prescription for an opioid, compared to an average of 18 percent in Kentucky. It should be noted that hydrocodone is only his third most common prescription, that it is the only opioid in his top ten number of prescribed drugs, and only 3 percent of his overall prescriptions.

However, it should also be noted that he is ranked sixteenth on the list of prescribers of hydrocodone-acetaminophen in the nation, using the Medicare data, and the second highest prescriber of the medication among family practitioners in the nation.

Furthermore, it's a matter of public record that in 2013, the Kentucky medical board filed a complaint against Richard for prescribing excessive amounts and combinations of addictive drugs. The case settled when Richard agreed to pay a $7,500 fine and, among other things, maintain a drug log.

Between 2013 and 2015, Richard wrote 28,099 opioid prescriptions for his 3,318 patients. Each year, his volume of prescriptions increased noticeably even though the number of patients he treated with opioid drugs only rose slightly.

Our researcher signed in, told them he was from out of state and doing self-pay and that he pulled a muscle in his back. He waited the usual 30 minutes or so past the appointment time and was taken to the back to provide vitals and a urine sample, which is required in the state of Kentucky for all narcotic prescriptions.

Richard is a tall, charismatic man who wears worn but high-quality cowboy boots, and his greying hair just a little longer than military specs. He's got an "aw shucks" charm, four grown sons, a wife who works in Texas, and his own horse farm. From what we hear from other people complaining about their doctors, Richard seems to take more time to just talk and get to know you than the usual GP. He seems like a genuinely nice and caring fellow.

Our researcher explained that he was in the area temporarily for work, is self-employed and self-paying, and that he has lower back pain. Richard explained that this is probably temporary, wrote prescriptions for muscle relaxers and a narcotic pain reliever, and said that if it persists he will get our researcher a referral to pain management along with the documentation required.

We don't want to be unfair, but when he went into the part about getting a referral his pace and cadence went from good old boy actual engagement to what sounded like rote recitation. The documentation required to prescribe narcotics is specific and tedious.

And just like that, we had a prescription for 15 hydrocodone 10mg. Plus a free sample of high dose ibuprofen, and some legitimate advice on stretching and exercise.

As far as we know, nothing Richard provided our researcher in terms of care or advice was outside the prescribed scope of practice. We're not qualified to judge that. But it was just that easy. Really, really easy. Despite being from out-of-state. Despite presenting no insurance. Despite complaining of a simple pulled muscle. And all we needed to do for a referral to a pain clinic was to visit again. His office would provide the charts, and then we would just need to pay a nominal upfront fee and a monthly charge to a clinic.

Yes, there are plenty of reputable and ethical pain clinics, but every drug court judge and cop we've spoken to also showed us that there is no shortage of these new pill mills. They just take a few extra steps and cost a little extra money.

Those who are addicted or dependent are willing to go through the steps. And the dealers in white coats are happy to take the money. That's how the game is played. Even when just days before, the federal government executed the largest opioid-related bust of health care providers in history. We're led to conclude that even significant efforts by law enforcement do not scare physicians away from prescribing opiates, because they know that even a thin veneer of justification is sufficient to make enforcement impossible or prohibitively difficult.

10
The Big Bad

King of Prussia is a township on the outer edge of Philadelphia, a mix of high-end homes along with destination retail and class A office space at the convergence of four major highways.

Founded by Quakers in the early 1700s, it is adjacent to Valley Forge, where General George Washington and his ragtag Continental Army spent the brutal winter of 1777–1778. Washington's headquarters still stands. Tourists can walk about in the three story farmhouse, sliding their hand along the very stairway bannister that Washington would have touched daily for those lonely and harsh six months he and his men were encamped.

It puts one in touch with the rich history of America, and the strength of the men who fought for, founded, and built this country.

At the same time, today, the descendants of those patriots are under attack by a chemical weapon, here in the very shadow of this valley.

This is where we met Adam and his son Joshua. Both father and son have struggled with addiction. Their tale is somewhat different from some of the other folks we met in Appalachia. Adam and his family live in a very posh neighborhood just a few miles from Valley Forge National Park. Adam is a medical doctor in the area, and for obvious personal and professional reasons, we are keeping his family identity confidential.

Adam is a slender man in his early fifties with piercing green eyes and a cautious demeanor. Joshua, in his early twenties, shares his father's eyes and build. He's an engineering student at an Ivy League university nearby.

Father and son share something besides their appearance. They share an addiction to opioids.

We're at their house for the better part of a warm June day. It's spacious and well appointed, in a classic style befitting the community. Adam's wife serves us iced tea from a silver tray. Their family has roots in the area here that go back before Civil War. They're deeply involved in the community and donors to the arts in Philadelphia. They don't want to get more specific than that. The circles they run in are, in the end, a small world.

"I took a bad fall cycling," Adam says, his wife settling warmly beside him on their large leather couch. Josh, in a navy golf shirt, sits on an ottoman. "I had to have surgery on my knee. Despite decades of practice, I'd never actually had to take any kind of painkiller stronger than ibuprofen.

"The first day after I was foggy, but by the second or third day I was really looking forward to my next dose. You'd think of all people I would have known what was happening, but it's like it triggers something in you that short-circuits your logic and your knowledge. It's like I knew what was happening and just didn't care. I enjoyed the sense of well-being too much. And after all, I'm a doctor. I would know exactly my limits," he snorts, self-derisively.

"Six months later and I was taking five Vicodin a day, and having to cover my tracks for some pretty shady tactics I was using to get them," he says.

Adam considers himself lucky. It was his wife, not the state board or any controlling authority, that confronted him about his abuse of opioids. "She saved me," he says. Adam checked himself into a high-end recovery clinic that specializes in helping medical professionals who have addiction issues. After a month, he says he was clean. But he still attends NA meetings twice a week with Joshua.

As a junior in college, Joshua fell into abusing Adderall, as many students do. The energy and focus he got from its use left him with powerful headaches that lasted days. His fraternity brothers came through for him, hooking him up with a steady supply of opioid pills.

"It didn't take long for me to go from using them for headaches to using them for fun," he says.

After Adam had returned from rehab, he told his family about his addiction. That's when Joshua realized that if a man he so admired and was as strong as his father could succumb to addiction, then surely he had already.

"It was the hardest thing in the world to tell my dad, days after he was out of rehab, that I was addicted as well," Joshua tells us. Joshua joined an out-patient program close to his parent's home and that summer he too got clean.

"The thing is, and what makes me angry about it when I let it, is that through rehab and meetings, both my son and I are in recovery, but we will always be addicted. We'll never be sure that we won't ever have a moment of weakness again. We'll have to always be on guard. And our worst fear is that some injury might befall one of us, and that we'll have to face the possibility of needing pain medications," Adam says. "Nothing can ever make us whole."

* * *

Some believe that civil suits, including the large-scale class action lawsuits filed by states attorneys, may be the way to restore justice and bring the perpetrators of this crime to heel. The lawsuits filed by states, counties, and municipalities are today too numerous to recount here. Many have been combined into multi-jurisdictional lawsuits and class actions. But as we saw even as we were finishing this book, justice is elusive because it comes with a price—and Big Pharma is nothing if not well heeled.

While the Sackler tribe and their multinational, Purdue Pharma, are considered the white whale of this white blizzard of prescriptions and pills, the defendants in these state, regional, county and municipal suits include McKesson Corporation, Cardinal Health, AmerisourceBergen,   Janssen Pharmaceuticals (a subsidiary of Johnson & Johnson), Endo International, Teva Pharmaceutical of Israel, Allergan (formerly Actavis), Watson Pharmaceuticals, and Covidien.

There were some initial results from the lawsuits in the late 2010s. In mid-2019, Purdue Pharma settled with Oklahoma to pay $270 million rather than face trial on charges of illegal marketing practices and misrepresentation regarding the drug OxyContin, according to company and state press releases.

The Oklahoma settlement was announced in 2019 about two months before the state trial against Purdue Pharma and three other pharmaceutical companies was slated to begin, according to the Oklahoma Attorney General's office.

At that time, David L. Noll, associate professor of law at Rutgers Law School, was interviewed by the healthcare website Healio, where he said the decision to settle was likely driven by the fear the Sackler family members themselves would be called to testify. Being a civil trial where Fifth Amendment protections aren't guaranteed, Sackler family members could have been compelled to give self-incriminating testimony, which could open them up to criminal and further civil liability.

"The settlement seems driven by the imminent court date and the possibility that members of the Sackler family, who owns Purdue Pharma, would be called to testify," he told the journal.

That settlement in 2019 took the heat off the Sacklers at the time, but the pressure was mounting from the innumerable other class action lawsuits either filed at the time or in the works.

"The company will take advantage of the lull between trials to work on a global settlement of opioids cases," Noll continued in the interview with Healio.

"It will work with plaintiffs' attorneys and state attorneys general to determine how much total compensation is owed, who funds the settlement, and when settlement funds are paid."

It's not for nothing that Purdue Pharma is often thought of as the Big Bad in this whole, multi-decade affair.

The New Yorker reported in 2017 that OxyContin had generated Purdue Pharma more than $35 billion in sales in the twenty years since its release in 1995. The company's annual revenues at the time were about $3 billion, largely from OxyContin. The Sackler family was, according to varying estimates, worth between $13 and $14 billion in terms of their personal fortune.

The lawsuits against Purdue Pharma, as well as the other corporate pushers, detail strikingly similar allegations.

While we have focused on the human toll in terms of individual lives, families, and communities—much of which can't be labeled with a price tag—various plaintiffs against the industry allege that the actual toll can be measured in the tens of billions of dollars, when such costs as treatment facilities, law enforcement, criminal justice and courts, jail and prison, and the cost to hospitals and healthcare facilities are all taken into account.

According to the U.S. National Institutes of Health, the aggregate cost of all these factors—deaths, overdose, treatment, criminal justice—was $78.5 billion a year as of 2013, and it only grew from there as overdoses, use, abuse and treatment costs rose.

The complaints detailed in the various plaintiff cases allege basic patterns of malfeasance and more: distributors violated the federal Controlled Substances Act, because they were required to alert the U.S. Drug Enforcement Administration of any large, suspicious opioids purchases; manufacturers exaggerated the benefits of the opioids, knew doctors were being too free with prescriptions, and mislead or failed to inform doctors of how addictive opioids were; and big manufacturing companies lobbied politicians and the medical industry—including individual doctors—in an effort to artificially boost the prescribing of opioids.

This is by no means a comprehensive list of the allegations in the hundreds of lawsuits filed in the late 2010s, many of which are still active, but that is the general theme.

Individual companies face specific allegations, few as seemingly nefarious as the ones leveled against Purdue Pharma. As was alleged and established in court, Purdue Pharma marketed their opioids such as Oxycontin as less addictive than other painkillers and further claimed that they would last for twelve hours. (They did not, and commonly users would simply take more.)

If there was hope to be found in lawsuits, one might think that earlier lawsuits going back to the 2000s would have had an impact. For instance, in 2007, Purdue pled guilty to the federal offense of misbranding OxyContin "with intent to defraud and mislead the public." For that alone it paid a fine of $635 million, but it continued with business as usual, according to *The New York Times.*

That may seem like a steep fine, but consider this. As we detailed, Purdue received FDA approval to sell OxyContin in 1995. The following year it has gross sales of $45 million for the product. By 2002, Purdue was moving $1.5 billion in pills.

By 2007, $635 million was pocket change to the Sacklers.

It was all about the marketing.

The National Institutes of Health produced an after action report in 2009, which detailed what happened between 1996 and 2001. The following information is taken from that detailed report.

In the five years after OxyContin was brought to market, Purdue held more than forty national pain management conferences at swanky resorts in California and Florida, where Purdue hosted more than 5,000 doctors, nurses and pharmacists, generously covering all expenses at these luxury getaways. NIH notes that while medical professionals claim they are not influenced in their standards of care or medical treatments, it is well-documented that indeed they are.

And this wasn't just simple tit for tat. NIH says Purdue developed a sophisticated, tailored marketing approach geared towards individual physicians, building entire databases to hone their efforts.

According to the NIH report:

One of the critical foundations of Purdue's marketing plan for OxyContin was to target the physicians who were the highest prescribers for opioids across the country. The resulting database would help identify physicians with large numbers of chronic-pain patients. Unfortunately, this same database would also identify which physicians were simply the most frequent prescribers of opioids and, in some cases, the least discriminate prescribers.

A lucrative bonus system encouraged sales representatives to increase sales of OxyContin in their territories, resulting in a large number of visits to physicians with high rates of opioid prescriptions, as well as a multifaceted information campaign aimed at them. In 2001, in addition to the average sales representative's annual salary of $55,000, annual bonuses averaged $71,500, with a range of $15,000 to nearly $240,000. Purdue paid $40 million in sales incentive bonuses to its sales representatives that year.

From 1996 to 2000, Purdue increased its internal sales force from 318 sales representatives to 671, and its total physician call list from approximately 33,400 to 44,500 to approximately 70,500 to 94,000 physicians. Through the sales representatives, Purdue used a patient starter coupon program for OxyContin that provided patients with a free limited-time prescription for a 7- to 30-day supply. By 2001, when the program was ended, approximately 34,000 coupons had been redeemed nationally.

This went so much farther than the typical pharma-branded swag that doctors were used to getting showered with—pens, golf clubs, fishing hats, and so on—though it was, according to the report, unprecedented for a schedule II narcotic.

What Purdue was pushing in these seminars was the idea that

there should be a more generous use of opioids, especially their time-release opioids. The NIH found that during and after the time of these marketing efforts, the number of primary care physicians prescribing OxyContin and other opioids rose dramatically. Previously, it seems, such strong painkillers were prescribed for treating patients dealing with post-op or post-trauma pain by specialists, who most likely had training in dealing with both pain management, chronic pain, and—critically—addiction issues related to opioids.

The NIH found that Purdue's push for OxyContin for more than just post-operative or cancer-related pain contributed directly to an increase by a factor of ten. The number of OxyContin prescriptions rose from 670,000 in 1997 to almost 6.2 million in 2002. Related to this was a four-fold increase in the prescription of the drug for cancer-related pain.

Not only was Purdue and its contemporaries aware of their actions, but so was the U.S. National Institutes for Health, the DEA, Health and Human Services, and the CDC.

They've been running this game for a long time, and those who were supposed to be the watchmen did just that—sat back and watched.

Not that Purdue was alone in all of this. In the runup to 2017, half a dozen companies including Purdue, McKesson, Mallinckrodt, Costco Wholesale, and Cardinal Health settled in small amounts ranging from $11.75 million to $150 million for various patterns detailed above, such as failing to report suspicious orders, improperly filling prescriptions, providing unconscionably large orders at state-wide levels, and more.

In one case, in 2017, Cardinal Health settled for $20 million with the state of West Virginia for the company's distribution of opioids in the state between 2007 and 2012.

"Cardinal and other wholesalers in a six-year period sent 780 million hydrocodone and oxycodone pills to West Virginia—433 per state resident. In that time, there were 1,728 fatal overdoses from the addictive painkillers," stated a 2018 Congressional hearing.

Few believe these lawsuits will harm Big Pharma, even if the settlement amounts were ten or one hundred times larger. Decades after the Big Tobacco settlements, those companies are still in business. The executives behind those companies are still in business. Most of all, the settlements reached included agreements that the executives, those who told the lies and whose addictive products killed millions, would be immune from criminal prosecution or personal liability. Pacific Gas and Electric is still in business, despite Erin Brockovich. Yes, it's likely that damages and awards could run into the billions, but for many of these companies, that's just a minor setback.

Perhaps most importantly, little money from these lawsuits will ever work its way down to the people who were victimized by the opioid plague, whether it's coal workers in West Virginia, or Adam and Josh in King of Prussia.

Big Tobacco settlements did not end up being spent to help the victims of malicious tobacco advertising. In 2013, NPR reported that most of the tobacco settlement money disappeared into the coffers of state governments without any strings attached. Little of it was earmarked for anti-smoking efforts and almost none to provide health care for smokers. Instead, the majority was made available to lawmakers to spend as they pleased. According to NPR, "Colorado has spent tens of millions of its share to support a literacy program, while Kentucky has invested half of its money in agricultural programs."

The reality is that as well-intentioned as the state lawsuits may be, they end up being a way for corporate criminals to avoid facing those they most directly harmed. In exchange for giant settlements that end up in the hands of politicians, corporations and their executives receive amnesty from individual lawsuits that would otherwise arise as a result of their malfeasance.

And the end result is that very little changes at the street level. Smoking kills you eventually, but it rarely destroys your life the way that opiates do. Entire communities are not decimated by tobacco. Tobacco users who are denied access to Marlboros do not turn to taking drugs by injection in order to get their fix. And yet, we are using the same formula to fight the purveyors of this poison that we unsuccessfully used to attack tobacco companies.

11
Lawyers, Drugs, and Money

Want to know why political policies and solutions failed? Consider the following statistics from the Center for Public Integrity:

- *Drug companies and allied advocates spent more than $880 million on lobbying and political contributions at the state and federal level over the past decade; by comparison, a handful of groups advocating for opioid limits spent $4 million. The money covered a range of political activities important to the drug industry, including legislation and regulations related to opioids.*
- *The opioid industry and its allies contributed to roughly 7,100 candidates for state-level offices.*
- *The drug companies and allied groups have an army of lobbyists averaging 1,350 per year, covering all 50 state capitals.*
- *The opioid lobby's political spending adds up to more than eight times what the formidable gun lobby recorded for political activities during the same period.*
- *For over a decade, a group called the Pain Care Forum has met with some of the highest-ranking health officials in the federal government, while quietly working to influence proposed regulations on opioids and promote legislation and reports on the problem of untreated pain. The group is coordinated by the chief lobbyist for Purdue Pharma, the maker of OxyContin.*

- *Two of the drug industry's most active allies, the American Cancer Society Cancer Action Network and the Academy of Integrative Pain Management, have contacted legislators and other officials about opioid measures in at least 18 states, even in some cases when cancer patients were specifically exempted from drug restrictions. State lawmakers often don't know that these groups receive part of their funding from drug makers.*

- *Five states have passed laws related to abuse-deterrent opioids and scores of bills have been introduced, with at least 21 using nearly identical language that some legislators said was supplied by pharmaceutical lobbyists. Pharmaceutical companies lobby for such laws, which typically require insurers and pharmacists to give preferential treatment to the patent-protected drugs, even though some experts say the deterrents are easily circumvented.*

So it's pretty obvious they've gamed the political remedy. Those politicians that Big Pharma haven't bought outright, they've managed to hoodwink with concern troll-style doubletalk—helping to write the very rules and regulations that they want in the guise of fighting the opioid crisis and delivering better patient care. By spreading their tentacles around Washington, DC and state capitols across the country, Big Pharma has made it well-nigh impossible for any actual regulatory crackdown, or even oversight with any teeth.

Surely, then, the courts could offer a solution?

After all, as we noted in the previous chapter, there have been hundreds of cases brought against Big Pharma, with some measures of victory. But the victories, in terms of the dollar amounts, the damage to corporate reputation, and the imposition of judicial orders in lieu of regulatory crackdown, have been picayune. Ultimately they have slowed the pace of the opioid industry juggernaut about as much as bugs splatting on the windshield slows a tractor trailer on the highway.

In the latter half of the 2000s and into the 2010s, as the opioid epidemic consumed the American landscape, states and the US Department of Justice began the long slog of bringing lawsuits against Purdue Pharma and the Sacklers. The damage just couldn't be ignored any more. A flood of lawsuits followed from municipalities and others. Eventually most of them were combined under a single umbrella in U.S. Bankruptcy Court.

And this is where it became a case "full of sound and fury, signifying nothing," to quote *Macbeth*.

Because when you look at the big legal decision against Purdue Pharma that was announced in late August 2021, even as we were finishing this book, it became clear that there is no judicial will to bring justice against the perpetrators of this crime.

"Purdue Pharma Is Dissolved and Sacklers Pay $4.5 Billion to Settle Opioid Claims" reads *The New York Times* headline of September 1st, 2021.

"The ruling in bankruptcy court caps a long legal battle over the fate of a company accused of fueling the opioid epidemic and the family that owns it," declares the secondary headline.

The news would appear grim for the Sackler tribe and Purdue Pharma, if the story were taken at face value.

Under the terms of the deal reached in U.S. Bankruptcy Court in White Plains, New York, Judge Robert Drain ruled that Purdue Pharma was dissolved as a corporate entity, and that the owners and the Sackler family would pay more than $4.5 billion in fines, fees and restitution. That money is supposed to be paid out throughout this decade, with the lion's share coming from the former Purdue entity and from projected profits of the "public interest" drug company that will emerge from Purdue's corpse.

The king is dead, long live the king, it seems. It is also a cruel twist that the new company will focus on making drugs to fight opioid addiction. First they sold America the disease, then they get to sell America the cure for that disease.

The details of the agreement and order provide that Purdue agreed to plead guilty in federal court to three counts of felony conspiracy to violate the Food, Drug and Cosmetic Act and the Federal Anti-Kickback Statute. The penalties under the deal include a $3.5 billion criminal fine and $2 billion in criminal forfeiture, the former of which is to be paid out in installments through 2030.

That's it. That's the extent of their criminal charges—violating business laws and regulations. And while Purdue must make public some thirty million documents, emails, and records that detail some elements of Purdue's role in the opioid crisis, it won't reveal the full extent of their malfeasance.

A few emails that have been made public in the course of the bankruptcy trial already are pretty damning, as reported by *STAT News,* with links to the full documents included.

In one email exchange dating back to January 1997, Purdue executives were hyper-concerned about Merck Medco, the national pharmacy benefit management firm, which was warning doctors that using OxyContin for chronic pain treatment could lead to addiction and abuse.

Richard Sackler told executives in the email chain that such concerns about addiction had to be "obliterated" as it threatened their move into the non-cancer pain management space:

> *I think that [Dr.] Paul [Goldenheim] has a good point, but we should consider that "addiction" may be a convenient way to "just say 'NO'" and when this objection is obliterated, they will fall back on the question of cost. Unless we can give a convincing presentation that [Purdue's] products are less prone to addiction potential, abuse or diversion than [other opioid] products. I think this can be done, but I defer to BK [Dr. Robert Kaiko] and RR [Dr. Robert Reder] and other experts.*

In another email going back to 1996, the year OxyContin was brought to market, Sackler told executives that he wanted to highlight Purdue's dogged willingness to fight any patent infringement by competitors so that the company would be "feared as a tiger with claws, teeth and balls."

Another email exchange between Sackler and Michael Friedman, head of sales and marketing, came in 1997, where Friedman told Sackler that there was a false impression among physicians that OxyContin wasn't as strong as morphine and that he didn't want to correct that misperception because it was helping sales.

"It would be extremely dangerous at this early stage in the life of the product to make physicians think the drug is stronger or equal to morphine," the email states. "We are well aware of the view held by many physicians that oxycodone is weaker than morphine. I do not plan to do anything about that,"

Sackler replied, "I agree with you."

Despite all this obvious, criminal intent, none of the executives are facing jail time.

"Purdue deeply regrets and accepts responsibility for the misconduct detailed by the Department of Justice," said Purdue Chairman Steve Miller, who joined the company leadership in July 2018, just before Purdue filed for bankruptcy.

As for the Sackler family? They are separately on the hook for—wait for it—just $225 million.

This for a family with a current estimated net worth of between $11 billion and $13 billion, which during these suits revealed they had personally moved $1.36 billion into offshore—and therefore untouchable—accounts, according to court records from this very same bankruptcy court, which Judge Drain specifically addressed in his ruling, according to *The New York Times* coverage of the judge's decision. In fact, it's suspected that the Sacklers transferred more than $10 billion out of the company between 2008 and 2017, as scrutiny of the company increased. Via *The New York Times:*

"This is a bitter result," he said. "B-I-T-T-E-R," he spelled out, explaining that he was frustrated that so much Sackler money was parked in offshore accounts. He said he had expected and wished for a higher settlement.

This deal has been in the works since October 2020, when the US Department of Justice announced the proposed terms of its "global resolution of its criminal and civil investigations into the opioid manufacturer Purdue Pharma LP, and a civil investigation into the individual shareholders from the Sackler family," according to an October 21, 2020 press release from the Justice Department.

The release provides seemingly damning quotes from then-Deputy Attorney General Jeffrey Rosen:

"The abuse and diversion of prescription opioids has contributed to a national tragedy of addiction and deaths, in addition to those caused by illicit street opioids," said Deputy Attorney General Jeffrey A. Rosen. "With criminal guilty pleas, a federal settlement of more than $8 billion, and the dissolution of a company and repurposing its assets entirely for the public's benefit, the resolution in today's announcement re-affirms that the Department of Justice will not relent in its multi-pronged efforts to combat the opioids crisis."

The FBI weighed in as well. Steven M. D'Antuono, Assistant Director in Charge of the FBI Washington Field Office, tossed around phrases about violations of the law, and "seeking justice":

Purdue, through greed and violation of the law, prioritized money over the health and well-being of patients. The FBI remains committed to holding companies accountable for their illegal and inexcusable activity and to seeking justice, on behalf of the victims, for those who contributed to the opioid crisis.

In fact the press release specifically states that "These resolutions do not include the criminal release of any individuals, including members of the Sackler family, nor are any of the company's executives or employees receiving civil releases."

Strong words. And just words, because Judge Drain's order does exactly what the Justice Department said the agreement wouldn't do—protect the Sackler family and Purdue executives.

The Sacklers, according to the judge's order, are absolved from Purdue's liability. That's why they are only on the hook for $225 million and why they will get to maintain their elite status as one of the richest families in the United States.

While some states that are party to the settlement said they would fight this agreement in appellate court, most accepted the terms, even though the ruling with its fines and fees and penalties doesn't even begin to cover the monetary cost of the opioid crisis, to say nothing of addressing the concept of justice for the hundreds of thousands who died.

If it stands, the settlement is the end of the road for the bulk of the thousands of lawsuits against Purdue, and therefore the end of legal means for extracting justice. The Sacklers, who never filed for bankruptcy, are being given the same civil protections as if they did, while barely having to give what amounts to about 2 percent of their reported net worth. Two. Percent.

Oh, and they have seven years to make good on the payments.

"The DOJ failed," Maura Healey, attorney general for Massachusetts, told *The New York Times* in October 2020, after the proposed settlement was announced. She goes on:

Justice in this case requires exposing the truth and holding the perpetrators accountable, not rushing a settlement to beat an election. I am not done with Purdue and the Sacklers, and I will never sell out the families who have been calling for justice for so long.

The Sacklers have, to this day, never admitted wrong-doing.

Of course, the Sacklers and Purdue are not the only villains in this story. Endo International, Mallinckrodt, Teva Pharmaceuticals of Israel, Johnson & Johnson, Janssen, Knight Therapeuticals, Cardinal, McKesson, AmerisourceBergen, WalMart, CVS, Walgreens, and other drug manufacturers and distributors are facing civil actions filed by more than 2,500 jurisdictions in state and federal courts.

While states and municipalities filed to recover costs associated with the opioid epidemic, individuals and their families are filing lawsuits to recover damages caused by addiction and the loss of loved ones who overdosed. The Sacklers and Purdue may be off the menu, but the rest of the manufacturers and distributors are not.

And it's not hard to see what kind of justice they can expect, given the way the Sacklers skated.

A large share of the outstanding lawsuits were consolidated before a federal judge in Cleveland, Ohio. That judge, U.S. District Judge Dan Polster, ruled that the cases may proceed to trial but has pushed similarly for a "global" settlement, not unlike Purdue's, to resolve all the suits.

Plaintiffs do not support this move, but Big Pharma does—easier to deal with one judge and jury than thousands.

12
Let Justice Be Done

As we close our investigation into this crime that has been perpetrated, questions remain. How did this happen? And who is the guilty party?

We've dug through a lot of data. We've met a lot of people and listened to their stories. We've been to the crime scene and examined it in grim and tragic detail.

This was a murder. But it's also a chemical weapons attack. Not by a hostile foreign nation, but by those most entrusted to protect, serve and heal America.

So who is guilty? The doctors? The pharmacists? The regulators? The manufacturers? The distributors? The pharmaceutical companies?

The fact is, it's everyone. Every last one of them. Like the passengers in Agatha Christie's *Murder on the Orient Express,* every one of them had a hand in this.

From top to bottom and from start to finish, all it would have taken is one actor to do more than raise a red flag or start a campaign to "raise awareness." Any one of them could have prevented this before it started, or stopped it after it was in motion, by blowing the whistle hard and by refusing to cooperate with what everyone knew was going on.

Pharmaceutical companies manufactured phony reports that claimed their products were safe and non-addictive, much like Big Tobacco did decades ago, and just as dishonestly. They created products they knew would have patients—customers—coming back and literally begging for more. They manufactured and distributed these products—this poison—in insane amounts that no one, at any level, could have thought made sense.

Regulators at the FDA green-lit these products and hand-waved any concerns raised by the blatantly obvious fact that opiates, opioids, and synthetic opioid derivatives are highly addictive. They accepted as research what were overtly dishonest marketing materials. Deregulation became their highest totem.

The medical field as a whole bought into the pain management and "pain as a fifth vital sign" malarkey that was bought and paid for by Big Pharma. The industry took as read the propaganda that Purdue and others manufactured.

Doctors at every level failed in their due diligence and their duty to their patients. They accepted almost blindly the marketing of these drugs. Individually, they were, at best, derelict in their duty to their patients and, at worst, complicit in the money-making scheme hatched by the manufacturers.

Pharmacists and pharmacies filling prescriptions for tens of millions of pills in towns with populations that number in the thousands were also culpable. While many may hide behind the idea of "duty to fill," they couldn't help but see what was really happening. Those that weren't actively in on this crime could have done something to bring it to the attention of state or federal regulators or authorities.

Government's first role is to protect the people of the nation. Legislators were either ignorant or indifferent to the suffering of their constituents for decades. The executive branch's regulatory and law enforcement apparatus either rubber-stamped manufacturers and doctors, or made it such a low priority that this cancer grew unabated. State licensing boards were more interested in protecting their members—doctors or pharmacists—than they were in protecting the public or upholding professional standards.

And let's not leave out the victims, the way all of the above did.

In parts of this country, it's almost impossible to find someone not directly or indirectly impacted by the opioid plague, which is so potent that it has even reached middle- and upper-class suburbs and their veneer of composure. But let's face the fact that the majority of this crime was perpetrated on and aimed at one specific group of Americans: rural and working-class Whites, primarily in Appalachia and the South, the people no one in power has time for or wants to represent, the people it's most politically frowned upon to speak for or identify with. It's not a coincidence that they suffered for so long unheard.

To hammer home the point that it wasn't just simple greed or supply and demand market forces but actual malice that led to Big Pharma spreading their poisons in rural, working-class, White America, consider emails that came to light recently in the spring of 2021, reported by *Mountain State Spotlight*. Senior executives at one of the largest American drug distributors circulated rhymes and emails mocking "hillbillies" who had become addicted to opioid painkillers even as the company poured hundreds of millions of pills into parts of Appalachia at the heart of the opioid epidemic.

In a 2001 email, long before the peak of opioid overdose deaths, one senior executive at a pharmaceutical distribution firm used the theme song to the old TV sitcom "The Beverly Hillbillies," mocking Jed, "a poor mountaineer" who "barely kept his habit fed." According to the re-tasked lyrics, "Jed" travels to Florida to buy "Hillbilly Heroin," the nickname, as we saw in our travels, for OxyContin.

Another verse of the parody song described Kentucky as "OxyContinVille." Further, when Kentucky's legislature approved new rules and regulations to try to fight the opioid crisis in the Bluegrass state, AmerisourceBergen executive Chris Zimmerman wrote, "One of the hillbilly's [sic] must have learned how to read."

Easily among the most infuriating, one email from a

pharmaceutical executive contained a fake breakfast cereal box for the product "Sugar Smacks" with the word "smack" under the words "OxyContin for kids."

Zimmerman was back again with what he must have thought was a knee-slapper, after Florida started cracking down on pill mills. His email to peers read, "Watch out Georgia and Alabama there will be a max exodus of Pillbillies heading north."

A superficially recalcitrant Zimmerman said in court, according to press coverage of the trial, that he regretted sending the emails but that it reflected the environment at the time.

There absolutely was conscious malice against working-class, White people in rural America.

These are the victims. We have heard their stories. They deserve to be made whole. They deserve justice.

Where is the corporate death penalty for those companies that wrought this injustice on the nation? Why aren't the executives behind this being frog-marched by U.S. Marshals into criminal trials? Why aren't doctors and pharmacists who stood idly by or actively engaged in this crime having their licenses yanked permanently? Whatever happened to "first, do no harm"?

Why is it that millions of lives can be destroyed, hundreds of thousands killed, families sundered and no one is held criminally accountable?

Who speaks for these people?

Where is justice?

Bibliography

Note: Much of the information in this book was sourced directly from interviews conducted by the authors. The following is a selected bibliography for referenced material and statistics as well as encouraged reading.

Chapter 1: Lost in America

Centers for Disease Control and Prevention. "Prescription Opioid Overdose Death Maps." Accessed July 14, 2021. https://www. cdc.gov/drugoverdose/deaths/prescription/ maps.html

"Combating the Opioid Epidemic: Examining Concerns about Distribution and Diversion." House Hearing before the Subcommittee on Oversight and Investigations of the Committee on Energy and Commerce. May 8, 2018. https://www.govinfo.gov/content/pkg/chrg-115hhrg31601/html/chrg-115hhrg31601.htm

Energy and Commerce Committee, Majority Staff. "Red Flags and Warning Signs Ignored: Opioid Distribution and Enforcement Concerns in West Virginia." December 19, 2018. https:// republicans-energycommerce.house.gov/wp-content/uploads/ 2018/12/Opioid-Distribution-Report-FinalREV.pdf

Gupta, Ruhal. *Opioid Response Plan for the State of West Virginia.* West Virginia Department of Health and Human Resources, January 30, 2018. https://dhhr.wv.gov/bph/Documents/ODCP% 20Response%20Plan%20Recs/Opioid%20Response%20Plan%20for%20t he%20State%20of%20West%20Virginia%20January%202018.pdf

Chapter 2: The Blizzard

Armstrong, David. "Drug maker thwarted plan to limit OxyContin prescriptions at dawn of opioid epidemic." *STAT News,* October 26, 2016. https://www.statnews.com/2016/10/26/oxycontin-maker-thwarted-limits/

Armstrong, David. "Former execs charged with bribing doctors to prescribe potent painkiller." *STAT News,* December 8, 2016. https://www.statnews.com/2016/12/08/insys-therapeutics-fentanyl-charges/

Blau, Max. "STAT forecast: Opioids could kill nearly 500,000 Americans in the next decade." *STAT News,* June 27, 2017. https://www.statnews.com/2017/06/27/opioid-deaths-forecast/

Centers for Disease Control and Prevention. *2019 Annual Surveillance Report of Drug-Related Risks and Outcomes—United States Surveillance Special Report. Centers for Disease Control and Prevention, U.S. Department of Health and Human Services.* November 1, 2019. https://www.cdc.gov/drugoverdose /pdf/ pubs/2019-cdc-drug-surveillancereport.pdf.

Commonwealth of Massachusetts v. Purdue Pharma L.P. "The Commonwealth's Pre-Hearing Memorandum for the Hearing Set for January 25, 2019." January 15, 2019. https://cdn.arstechnica.net/wp-content/uploads/2019/01/ Mass_AGO_Pre-Hearing_Memo_and_Exhibits-1.pdf

Crawford, Heather. "Florida now has one of the strictest opioid prescribing laws in the country." *First Coast News,* July 5, 2018. https://www.firstcoastnews.com/article/news/florida-now-has-one-of-the-strictest-opioid-prescribing-laws-in-the-country/77-571151370

Dolan, Kerry A. "Billion-Dollar Clans: America's 25 Richest Families 2016." *Forbes,* June 29, 2016. https://www.forbes.com/sites/kerryadolan/2016/06/29/billion-dollar-clans-americas-25-richest-families-2016/?sh=6d3516a832f5

Keefe, Patrick Radden. "The Family that Built an Empire of Pain." *New Yorker,* October 23, 2017. https://www.newyorker.com/magazine/2017/10/30/the-family-that-built-an-empire-of-pain

McGinnes, Meagan. "Police hope viral video of mother's overdose in Family Dollar sheds light on opioid epidemic." *Boston.com,* September 23, 2016. https://www.boston.com/news/local-news/2016/09/23/police-hope-viral-video-of-mothers-overdose-in-family-dollar-sheds-light-on-opioid-epidemic/

Ornstein, Charles and Tracy Weber. "American Pain Foundation Shuts Down as Senators Launch Investigation of Prescription Narcotics."

ProPublica, May 8, 2012. https://www.propublica.org/article/senate-panel-investigates-drug-company-ties-to-pain-groups

Park, Alice. "Life after Addiction." *Time* and *Mic*, accessed July 14, 2021. https://time.com/life-after-opioid-addiction/

Porter, Jane and Hershel Jick, letter to the editor. "Addiction Race in Patients Treated with Narcotics." *New England Journal of Medicine*, 302, no. 2 (January 1980): 123. https://www.nejm.org/doi/pdf/10.1056/NEJM198001103020221

Ross, Casey. "Behind the photo: How heroin took over an Ohio town." *STAT News,* September 21, 2016. https://www.statnews.com/2016/09/21/photo-heroin-ohio/

Chapter 3: A Town as a Corpse

ProPublica. "Prescriber Checkup: Sami Moizuddin M.D." Accessed July 14, 2021. https://projects.propublica.org/checkup/providers/ 1265453120

ProPublica. "Vital Signs: Samia Moizuddin M.D." Accessed July 14, 2021. https://projects.propublica.org/vital-signs/doctor/ 1265453120

Chapter 4: The Rot

Brill, Alex. "New state-level estimate of the economic burden of the opioid epidemic." American Enterprise Institute. *AEIdeas,* January 16, 2018. https://www.aei.org/health-policy/new-state-level-estimates-of-the-economic-burden-of-the-opioid-epidemic/

Centers for Disease Control and Prevention. "Drug Overdose Mortality by State." Accessed July 15, 2021. https://www.cdc.gov/nchs/pressroom/sosmap/drug_poisoning_mortality/drug_poisoning.htm

Hessler, Courtney. "Violent crime in Huntington drops 20 percent in 2018." *Associated Press*, December 23, 2018. https://apnews.com/article/2597fbc11a36400fb4382f8d4fb318ff

Pilcher, James, Liz Dufour, and Kate Murphy. "Trapped and trafficked: One town's dark secret." *The Cincinnati Enquirer*, March 21 2019, updated October 23, 2020. https://www. cincinnati.com/in-depth/news/2019/03/21/sex-trafficking-trapped-and-trafficked-portsmouth-ohio/2839816002/

Rogers, James. "Kentucky middle schoolers design 3-D printed device to help fight opioid crisis." *Fox News*, May 15, 2018, updated May 16, 2018. https://www.foxnews.com/tech/ kentucky-middle-schoolers-design-3d-printed-device-to-help-fight-opioid-crisis

The United States Attorney's Office, Middle District of Ohio. "Justice Department Files First of its Kind Action to Stop Tennessee Pharmacies' Unlawful Dispensing of Opioids." February 8, 2019. https://www.justice.gov/usao-mdtn/pr/justice-department-files-first-its-kind-action-stop-tennessee-pharmacies-unlawful

The United States Attorney's Office, Southern District of Ohio. "U.S. Attorneys Announce Initiative to Combat Violent Crime and Drug Trafficking in Tri-State Area." February 12, 2018. https://www.justice.gov/usao-sdoh/pr/us-attorneys-announce-initiative-combat-violent-crime-and-drug-trafficking-tri-state

Chapter 5: Fighting Back

Grossman, Dave. "On Sheep, Wolves and Sheepdogs." In *On Combat: The Psychology and Physiology of Deadly Conflict in War and in Peace.* WSG Research Publications, 2004.

Synan, Tom. "Chief: Why care about another dead addict?" *The Cincinnati Enquirer*, December 3, 2014. https://www.cincinnati.com/story/opinion/contributors/2014/12/03/chief-care-another-dead-addict/19830689/

Vaida, Bara. "Infectious disease outbreaks rise with opioid epidemic." *Association of Health Care Journalists,* August 27, 2018. https://healthjournalism.org/blog/2018/08/infectious-disease-outbreaks-rise-with-opioid-epidemic/

Warren, Beth. "Fentanyl killed 763 people in Kentucky - twice as many as heroin." *Courier Journal*, July 25, 2018. https://www. courier-journal.com/story/news/local/2018/07/25/louisville-kentucky-drug-deaths-fatal-overdoses-spike-crystal-meth-fentanyl-heroin-pain-pills-blamed/835740002/

Chapter 6: Never-Ending Battle

Entirely personal research

Chapter 7: Among the Culprits

Associated Press. "Doctors charged in West Virginia, Virginia pill mill case." *The Oklahoman,* February 20, 2016.
https://www.oklahoman.com/article/feed/1785631/doctors-charged-in-west-virginia-virginia-pill-mill-case

Eyre, Eric. "Drug firm exec to apologize for some opioid shipments to WV: 'I am deeply sorry.'" *Charleston Gazette-Mail,* May 7, 2018.
https://www.wvgazettemail.com/news/health/drug-firm-exec-to-apologize-for-some-opioid-shipments-to-wv-i-am-deeply-sorry/article_2a53ffc4-f20e-5ae8-84b1-c9018add27c.html

Centers for Disease Control and Prevention. "Opioid Painkiller Prescribing." Vital Signs. Last modified September 5, 2018.
https://www.cdc.gov/vitalsigns/opioid-prescribing/index.html

Centers for Disease Control and Prevention. "Prescription Opioid Overdose Death Maps." Drug Overdose. Last modified March 24, 2021.
https://www.cdc.gov/drugoverdose/deaths/prescription/ maps.html

Siemaszko, Corky. "Dr. Katherine Hoover, accused of fueling West Virginia's opioid crisis, still thinks she didn't do anything wrong." *NBC News,* September 25, 2018. https://www.nbcnews.com/ news/us-news/dr-katherine-hoover-accused-fueling-west-virginia-s-opioid-crisis-n909366

State of Ohio Board of Pharmacy. "Boardman Podiatrist Indicted on 79 Charges including Drug Trafficking." February 7, 2019.
https://pharmacy.ohio.gov/Documents/Pubs/NewsReleases/2019/Boardman%20Podiatrist%20Indicted%20on%2079%20Charges%20including%20Drug%20Trafficking.pdf

Chapter 8: Too Close to Home

Centers for Disease Control and Prevention. *Managing HIV and hepatitis C outbreaks among people who inject drugs: A guide for state and local health departments.* March 2018. https://www.cdc.gov/hiv/pdf/programresources/guidance/cluster-outbreak/cdchiv-hcv-pwid-guide.pdf

Ethridge, Maggie May. "This Is Exactly What Happens When You Overdose." Provided by Dr. Anthony Morocco. *VICE,* June 29, 2017. https://www.vice.com/en/article/a3dzyb/this-is-exactly-what-happens-when-you-overdose

Chapter 9: Doctor Feelgood

Centers for Disease Control and Prevention. "U.S. Opioid Dispensing Rate Maps." Drug Overdose. Last modified December 7, 2020. https://www.cdc.gov/drugoverdose/rxrate-maps/index.html

DeMio, Terry, Kevin Grasha, and Dan Horn. "Ohio, Kentucky doctors among 60 charged in pain pill bust acted 'like drug dealers.'" *The Cincinnati Enquirer,* April 17, 2019, updated April 18, 2019. https://www.cincinnati.com/story/news/2019/04/17/ opioid-pain-pill-federal-prescription-bust/3482202002/

Lord, Rich, and Maia Silber. "DEA is cracking down on physicians who overprescribe pills." *Pittsburgh Post-Gazette*, August 12, 2016. https://www.post-gazette.com/news/overdosed/2016/08/12/ Feds-have-taken-thousands-of-prescribing-licenses/stories/ 201608120095

National Institutes of Health. "Kentucky: Opioid-Involved Deaths and Related Harms." National Institute on Drug Abuse. Last modified April 3, 2020. https://www.drugabuse.gov/drug-topics/ opioids/opioid-summaries-by-state/kentucky-opioid-involved-deaths-related-harms

ProPublica. "Prescriber Checkup: John Richard M.D." Accessed July 15, 2021. https://projects.propublica.org/checkup/providers/ 1124047717

ProPublica. "Prescribers of HYDROCODONE-ACETAMINOPHEN in Kentucky." Accessed July 15, 2021. https://projects.propublica. org/checkup/drugs/1726/states/kentucky

The United States Attorney's Office, Western District of Tennessee. "U.S. Attorney Dunavant along with Federal, State and Local Partners Continue Efforts to Combat the Opioid Crisis." April 18, 2019. https://www.justice.gov/usao-wdtn/pr/us-attorney-dunavant-along-federal-state-and-local-partners-continue-efforts-combat

The United Stated Department of Justice, Office of Public Affairs. "Appalachian Regional Prescription Opioid (ARPO) Strike Force Takedown Results in Charges Against 60 Individuals, Including 53 Medical Professionals." April 17, 2019. https://www.justice.gov/opa/pr/appalachian-regional-prescription-opioid-arpo-strike-force-takedown-results-charges-against

United States of America v. Denver D. Tackett, DMD. April 11, 2019. https://www.justice.gov/opa/page/file/1155051/download

United States of America v. Elizabeth Korcz, M.D., Matthew Korcz, and Austin Haskew. March 28, 2019. https://www.justice.gov/opa/page/file/1155036/download

United States of America v. Ijaz Mahmood. April 3, 2019. https://www.justice.gov/opa/page/file/1154911/download

United States of America v. Marshall Plotka, MD. April 16, 2019. https://www.justice.gov/opa/page/file/1155371/download

United States of America v. Thomas Kelly Ballard III, M.D. April 15, 2019. https://www.justice.gov/opa/page/file/1155111/download

Chapter 10: The Big Bad

Associated Press. "Kentucky settles lawsuit with OxyContin maker for $24 million." *CBS News*, December 23, 2015. https://www.cbsnews.com/news/kentucky-settles-lawsuit-with-oxycontin-maker-for-24-million/

Bebinger, Martha. "Purdue Pharma Agrees To $270 Million Opioid Settlement With Oklahoma." *NPR*, March 26, 2019. https://www.npr.org/sections/health-hots/2019/03/26/706848006/purdue-pharma-agrees-to-270-million-opioid-settlement-with-oklahoma

Cardinal Health. "Cardinal Health Reaches Settlement With West Virginia. *PR Newswire*, January 9, 2017. https://www. prnewswire. com/newsreleases/cardinal-health-reaches-settlement-with-west-virginia-300387943.html

Department of Justice, Office of Public Affairs. "Costco Wholesale to Pay $11.75 Million to Settle Allegations of Lax Pharmacy Controls." January 19, 2017. https://www.justice.gov/opa/pr/costco-wholesale-pay-1175-million-settle-allegations-lax-pharmacy-controls

Department of Justice, Office of Public Affairs. "Mallinckrodt Agrees to Pay Record $35 Million Settlement for Failure to Report Suspicious Orders of Pharmaceutical Drugs and for Recordkeeping Violations." July 11, 2017. https://www.justice.gov/opa/pr/mallinckrodt-agrees-pay-record-35-million-settlement-failure-report-suspicious-orders

Department of Justice, Office of Public Affairs. "McKesson Agrees to Pay Record $150 Million Settlement for Failure to Report Suspicious Orders of Pharmaceutical Drugs." January 17, 2017. https://www.justice.gov/opa/pr/mckesson-agrees-pay-record-150-million-settlement-failure-report-suspicious-orders

Eban, Katherine. "OxyContin: Purdue Pharma's painful medicine." *Fortune*, November 9, 2011. https://fortune.com/2011/11/09/ oxycontin-purdue-pharmas-painful-medicine/

Florence, Curtis, et al. "The Economic Burden of Prescription Opioid Overdose, Abuse and Dependence in the United States, 2013." *Med Care*, 54, no. 10 (October 2016): 901-906. https://www.ncbi.nlm.nih.gov/pmc/articles/PMC5975355/

Hakim, Danny, Roni Caryn Rabin, and William K. Rashbaum. "Lawsuits Lay Bare Sackler Family's Role in Opioid Crisis." *New York Times*, April 1, 2019. https://www.nytimes.com/2019/04/ 01/health/sacklers-oxycontin-lawsuits.html

Meier, Barry. "In Guilty Plea, OxyContin Maker to Pay $600 Million." *The New York Times*, May 10, 2007. https://www.nytimes.com/2007/05/10/business/11drug-web.html

Morrell, Alex. "The OxyContin Clan: The $14 Billion Newcomer to Forbes 2015 List of Richest U.S. Families." *Forbes*, July 1, 2015. https://www.forbes.com/sites/alexmorrell/2015/07/01/the-oxycontin-clan-the-14-billion-newcomer-to-forbes-2015-list-of-richest-u-s-families/?sh=1b78d0e75e02

Noll, David L. "First opioid lawsuit settlement raises questions with dozens more cases waiting." Healio, April 3, 2019.

https://www.healio.com/news/primary-care/20190403/first-opioid-lawsuit-settlement-raises-questions-with-dozens-more-cases-waiting

NPR Staff. "15 Years Later, Where Did All The Cigarette Money Go?" *NPR*, October 13, 2013. https://www.npr.org/2013/10/13/ 233449505/15-years-later-where-did-all-the-cigarette-money-go

Van Zee, Art. "The Promotion and Marketing of OxyContin: Commerical Triumph, Public Health Tragedy." *Am J Public Health,* 99, no. 2 (February 2019): 221–227. https://www.ncbi.nlm.nih.gov/pmc/articles/PMC2622774/

Whyte, Liz Essley, Geoff Mulvihill, and Ben Wieder. "Politics of Pain: Drugmakers Fought State Opioid Limits Amid Crisis." *The Center for Public Integrity*, September 18, 2016, last updated December 15, 2016. https://publicintegrity.org/politics/state-politics/politics-of-pain-drugmakers-fought-state-opioid-limits-amid-crisis/

Chapter 11: Lawyers, Drugs and Money

The Center for Public Integrity and the Associated Press. "Pharma lobbying held deep influence over opioid policies." *The Center for Public Integrity,* September 18, 2016. https://publicintegrity.org/politics/state-politics/pharma-lobbying-held-deep-influence-over-opioid-policies/

Hoffman, Jan. "Purdue Pharma is Dissolved and Sacklers to Pay $4.5 Billion to Settle Opioid Claims." *The New York Times,* September 17, 2021. https://www.nytimes.com/2021/09/01/health/purdue-sacklers-opioids-settlement.html

Hoffman, Jan and Katie Benner. "Purdue Pharma Pleads Guilty to Criminal Charges for Opioid Sales." *The New York Times,* October 21, 2020. https://www.nytimes.com/2020/10/21/health/purdue-opioids-criminal-charges.html

Ross, Casey. "Purdue's Richard Sackler proposed plan to play down OxyContin risks, and wanted drug maker feared 'like a tiger,' files show." *STAT News,* December 2, 2019. https://www.statnews.com/2019/12/02/purdue-richard-sackler-proposed-plan-play-down-oxycontin-risks/

The United States Department of Justice, Office of Public Affairs. "Justice Department Announces Global Resolution of Criminal and Civil

Investigations with Opioid Manufacturer Purdue Pharma and Civil Settlement with Members of the Sackler Family." October 21, 2020. https://www.justice.gov/opa/pr/justice-department-announces-global-resolution-criminal-and-civil-investigations-opioid

Chapter 12: Let Justice Be Done

Manfield, Lucas and Lauren Peace. "As opioid epidemic raged, drug company executives made fun of West Virginians." *Mountain State Spotlight,* May 13, 2021. https://mountainstatespotlight.org/2021/05/13/opioid-company-executives-made-fun-of-west-virginians/

McGreal, Chris. "'Ground zero of the opioid epidemic': West Virginia puts drug giants on trial." *The Guardian,* May 3, 2021. https://www.theguardian.com/us-news/2021/may/03/us-opioid-crisis-west-virginia-drug-giants-trial

CPSIA information can be obtained
at www.ICGtesting.com
Printed in the USA
FSHW012211121121
86200FS